A BIGGER PICTURE

Memoir of a Military Artist

BENJAMIN RICHARD ADDISON

ISBN 978-1-63784-753-4 (paperback)
ISBN 978-1-63784-754-1 (digital)

Hawes & Jenkins Publishing
16427 N Scottsdale Road Suite 410
Scottsdale, AZ 85254
www.hawesjenkins.com

Printed in the United States of America

For My Family

INTRODUCTION

THIS IS A SHORT STORY about my dream of becoming an artist and realizing that the true brush strokes we make in life are not as individual artists, but it is the collective works of good people that fill in the vast canvas of God's masterpiece. My quest to become an artist turned out to be a search for meaning in my life and answering a calling to serve. I survived child abuse, bullies, and dangerous encounters overseas thanks to faith, prayer, and the many positive role models who guided me along the way. I look back on my short life through a new lens now. Now I see that my greatest accomplishments are providing for my family and helping others. Faith in God helped me to overcome challenges in an adventure of a lifetime.

I grew up in a small town. I could only dream of seeing the world. The military provided me with the means to travel abroad. I gained a type of education that cannot be found in traditional classrooms. Seeing our country through the eyes of others from far away enlightened me and gave me a new perspective to consider. How fortunate we are to live in the land of the free and the home of the brave. What a debt we owe to all those service members who sacrificed so much for us to have security.

I wish to thank my family for being so supportive of my service. They, too, sacrificed while I was away. Any success I enjoyed must be attributed to their love, patience, and understanding. Experiences changed who I am for better or worse, and for my family, it must be like getting to know someone new since I've come home. I hope that my story inspires others to believe in the power of prayer and serves as a light for those in the dark.

CHAPTER 1

A DIFFICULT BEGINNING

You will feel pain, but your pain
will turn to happiness.
—John 16:20

THE PATERNAL LINE OF MY Addison family tree can be traced seven generations ago to when Russell County pioneer Rodden Addison settled in Virginia from England. True to the family motto "To serve is to live," he patriotically served in the War of 1812, and many of his descendants lived to help others, such as Chris Addison, who was a Baptist minister. Unfortunately, as in many other families, we have had our share of tragedy caused mainly by the abuse of alcohol. In a drunken rage, my grandfather shot his wife and them himself, leaving my father among seven young children to grow up without a dad. My father married and had two children before I came along. His wife committed suicide and left my older half-siblings without a mom. Their childhood was hard and made worse by our father's alcohol addiction. Then he married my mother in 1973,

1

and I was born in Baltimore, Maryland, a year later. I was baptized at Christ Episcopal Church in the town of Forest Hill in Harford County, Maryland.

I grew up in northeastern Maryland, near the Pennsylvania state line. Inheritance money furnished a large new stone ranch house tucked away on thirteen acres of secluded property edged by more than a hundred freshly planted, bristling pine trees. Each of the children had our own bedroom. I wish we were closer, but a decade of difference in years and the fact that my mother could never replace theirs was a bitter one. I nevertheless looked up to them and wanted to be accepted. One of my earliest memories is of drawing pictures on napkins at the kitchen table. I must have been four or five years old when I watched my half brother scribble squares and other shapes while he was speaking with his girlfriend on the telephone. I was a little jealous that he was giving his attention to someone else. I grabbed a pen and a napkin at the kitchen table and thought I would draw something he would like. I drew a three-dimensional bulldozer at a construction site. It came naturally to me, and it looked like something an adult artist would render. He smiled when he saw my drawing. I realized the reward for doing art was to make people smile and feel good about what they see.

I knew then that I wanted to be an artist when I grew up. I found influence and inspiration for my artwork from superheroes and the military. My parents worked at the local US Army base known as Aberdeen Proving Ground in Harford County, Maryland. My mother was a secretary for engineers there, and when she couldn't get a babysitter for me, she took me to work with her. I was allowed to draw on blank office paper at an empty desk, where I drew pictures of tanks, ships, and aircraft for her coworkers. It felt good to see them pin up my artwork on bulletin boards in the office. I was in awe of seeing actual soldiers in their camouflaged uniforms with shiny black boots pass through the office. My mother was very proud, and she always made a point to introduce me to them.

The soldiers liked seeing me bring my toy soldiers to play with, and sometimes they knelt down to play with me on the carpet and correct my positioning of the tiny plastic tanks and Jeeps. Once on my birthday, a soldier leaned down and gave me five dollars! Each year for Armed Forces Day, the base would open its gates to the public and hold demonstrations, static displays of tanks, and Revolutionary War reenactments. I loved visiting the ordnance museum on the base because of the military toys for sale in the gift shop. After work, my parents would frequently bring home small gifts such as stickers, patches, and plastic army men. My bedroom was a sanctuary under the protection of toy soldiers, superheroes, and various stuffed animals. They served as models for the human form and animal shapes I drew in my sketch pad.

We didn't go to church. Looking back, I wish we did. I took my cues about morality from the influence of the military and from role models on television. Programs like "*Star Trek*," "*Batman*," and "*G.I. Joe*" aired each day after school, and Saturday mornings were for cartoon marathons. On Saturday nights, famous wrestling figures like Hulk Hogan preached to kids about the importance of "praying, working out, and taking their vitamins." The theme of good versus evil inspired my artwork. I practiced drawing every day. I created fantastic creatures and fairy tale worlds filled with soldiers protecting people and superheroes doing good deeds.

Those delicate first ten years of my childhood passed quickly. We hosted large family picnics where I played with my cousins, our aunts and uncles brought food, and everyone played softball. My grades were good in school, and I had good friends. Then everything changed when I was in the middle of fourth grade. Things began to fall apart at home. Financial pressures and suspicions of infidelity drove my parents to drink alcohol in excess, and they fought with each other often.

Their fighting was physical and very frightening. They slammed each other into the hallway walls outside my bedroom door and shouted profanity. I remember hiding behind a couch on the floor in the living room with my sketchbook and colored pencils. I drew my escape from the terror by inventing other worlds and characters that might fly in to save the day. I coped with the stress by hiding and sheltering in what seemed like safe places. The ability to draw what I could visualize in my mind was like having a special gift. I learned to recite the "Lord's Prayer" during a particularly bad night of our parents fighting.

> Dear Heavenly Father,
> Hallowed by thy name.
> Thy kingdom come, thy will be done,
> on Earth as it is in heaven.
> Give us this day our daily bread,
> and forgive us our trespasses as we forgive others
>   who trespass against us.
> Lead us not into temptation, but deliver us from
>   evil.
> For thine is the kingdom, the power, and the
>   glory, forever and ever. Amen.

I said this prayer over and over until I had it memorized. Saying it brought me a sense of peace and reassurance when I felt surrounded by turmoil. Calm and a sense of safety followed. Throughout my life, there have been many times I owed my sanity to being an artist and having faith in the power of prayer.

The divorce happened in 1984. My fourth-grade teacher, Mr. Smith, noted my artistic skills, but my grades in other subjects dropped. The ability to understand two- and three-point perspectives came easily to me, but I fell behind in mathematics, science, and English studies. My parents were no longer involved with my homework. I preferred to focus on creative projects like when the teacher asked us to write a story and draw pictures to accompany it. I created an elaborate series of images and cover art. We bound the small books with fabric and cardboard.

It was a routine day during the middle of the school year when the book project was almost finished. My mother came to the classroom suddenly to take me away. Mr. Smith protested at the lack of notice for withdrawing a student, but my mother would not hear of it. The other children in class were just as surprised as I was. She had me gather my things quickly because she wanted to hurry home to pack before my father came home from work. She was leaving him and taking me with her. It was heart-wrenching to suddenly say goodbye to my teacher, my friends, my bedroom, and everything I knew at home. I only had time to grab a few toys and clothes. The car kicked up rocks as we sped down the gravel driveway on our way to my mother's aunt's house.

Thirty minutes away lived my Great Aunt Bea in her early 1900s farmhouse. She had no children of her own, but she raised my mother and her siblings, rescuing them from neglectful and abusive parents. Now she was rescuing my mother again and me too by providing sanctuary for us during the divorce. My mother and I shared the guest bed upstairs. I was enrolled at a new elementary school. I missed my friends at my old school. The next year was filled with the drama of a custody and visitation battle. It felt like being stuck in a tug-of-war match. Each parent made their case for why I should live with them and demanded my loyalty over the others. I got sick with double pneumonia during the custody battle.

My mother made a habit of stopping at a bar to drink and meet men on her way home from work each day. I struggled with my homework, and my grades in school suffered. I dreaded my mother coming home drunk because she frequently wet the bed we shared. Eventually she met and married her next husband named Charlie, and we moved into a single-room apartment across the parking lot from the bar.

The tiny studio apartment was owned by the bar manager. It was convenient for my mother because she wouldn't have to drink and drive to get home. My school bus stop was the bar's main entrance, and the kids on the bus teased me every day because of it. I sat inside the bar at a booth and attempted to do my homework while waiting for my mother and Charlie to come and order my dinner from the bar's restaurant. The men's restroom at the bar was the first place I experienced being teased, touched, and taunted by drunken men. The second place was in the single-room apartment when Charlie climbed into my bed at night. I remember vividly the foul stench of his breath and his unwanted touching. I recited the Lord's Prayer that my brother taught me. I was bitter with God for the situation I found myself in. I missed what life was like before the divorce.

I began to withdraw from myself. The stress caused my esophagus to constrict, and I was unable to eat at times. I developed gastroesophageal reflux disease. I had no friends at the new school and felt too shy to get to know anyone. I was embarrassed by living next to a bar with alcoholic parents. I suffered mental, physical, and sexual abuse. Art was the only way I could escape from the torment at home. My grades dropped, and I failed to keep my attention in classes, with the exception of creative assignments. I drew pictures of places that I'd rather be. Sketches of superheroes were taped to the wall above my bed.

At the end of fifth grade, my mother and stepfather found a nicer two-bedroom apartment downtown. The city environment and new school offered a change of venue but introduced me to bullying. I was an outsider because I wasn't friends with anyone. I stayed quiet, doodling sketches at my desk before class began. I knew the other kids could never understand what it was like to have divorced parents. One day, a group of popular boys targeted me for my silence. I ignored their harsh jokes and remained silent, facing forward. I was anxious for the teacher to come in to start the class.

Wads of paper balls launched from behind me bounced off my shoulders. Slam! A heavy textbook hit the back of my head. I saw stars, and hot tears began to flow. I heard a boy say while laughing, "Look! He's crying like a baby." The teacher came in, and class began as if nothing had happened. Later that day at gym class, three of the boys circled me in the corner of the gymnasium while the other kids played basketball. They told me that one day after school, they would find me and stab me unless I fought them. I took their threat seriously and told the teacher and my mother when she got home after work. The teacher took no noticeable action. I was too terrified to go to school the next day. I give credit to my mother for going through the trouble to change my school district assignment.

I found myself at a safer school where I was welcomed by caring teachers and students. The new middle school even had its own planetarium and art classes as part of its curriculum. My mother changed her work schedule so that she could drive me to and from school. She knew that one of the ladies she worked with at the Army base was a black belt and also taught karate class near where we lived. There was only one other martial arts student, and we met twice a week to train. During the first month, I learned the vital fighting basics of keeping my balance and how to punch, kick, and block properly. We practiced defending against knife attacks, and I felt a sense of confidence to go back to riding the school bus on my own and being a latchkey kid again. The core teaching of karate class is that it is for self-defense only and not to use fighting skills recklessly. What I learned would be tested in real life one fateful night to protect my mother from domestic violence.

A few months went by since the bullying incident, and my mother and stepfather brought home their booze to drink from the liquor store. My mother preferred to drink whiskey mixed with soda until she consumed most of the bottle before passing out. Charlie enjoyed his case of beer. At least I had a door to my own bedroom that I could close. The door would not lock, but I managed to barricade it shut with my small hobby art desk and chair to keep Charlie from stumbling into my bed in his drunken stupor. My defenses didn't always hold. Even the protective line of stuffed animals along the outside edge of my bed bounced away helplessly when Charlie chose to lie in my bed instead of his own.

It was a Friday night when the fighting between Charlie and my mother escalated to its climax. The shouting and banging noises were louder than usual; then things suddenly got quiet. I opened my bedroom door to peek down the hall to the living room, where I saw Charlie leaning over my mother, strangling her with the neck strap of her nightgown. Mother's face was turning dark purple, and her eyes bulged wide. I raced down the hall in my underwear to try to save her.

I hit and kicked Charlie until he released his grip around my mother's throat. He stumbled and fell down. I helped my mother get up and out of the front door of the apartment. I followed behind her, and just like a scene from a horror movie, Charlie's hand came through the crack of the open doorway just in time to grab me by the waistband of my underwear and pull me back inside. My mother helped, and together, we pulled away from Charlie's grip. He slammed the door shut just in time for the police to arrive. A neighbor heard the ruckus and dialed 911. The police officers said that the best thing for us to do was to go somewhere else for the night and let Charlie recover from his hangover inside. We went to a shelter with my older half sister an hour away. My mother refused to leave Charlie despite the domestic violence, so I insisted on leaving her to go live with my father and stepmother.

Moving meant yet another change of school and presented new awkward challenges. I became socially isolated, and my grades dropped to barely passing. It wasn't long before I was subjected to a new form of abuse. Sexual abuse from my stepmother and my father stole away more innocence. I felt too ashamed and vulnerable to speak up and report it to anyone. From my previous experiences with bullies, I did not feel that anyone would care. I endured the abuse for two years until it was time to change schools again and move back in with my mother. She said she was finally leaving Charlie and getting a small house of her own away in the woods among rural Pennsylvania's Amish, just two houses away from my half sister's house.

It was only a matter of time before Charlie apologized to my mother for his behavior, and she took him in to live with us again. I was furious with my mother's decision, and I despised Charlie. I went to stay with my sister, who unexpectedly took on the role of parent for me. I slept on her couch and laid on the carpet behind it to hide and draw in my sketchbook. I was grateful for the shelter my sister provided, but I was once again affected by alcoholism because her husband turned into a different person when he drank.

CHAPTER 2

EARLY PARENTHOOD

I am the bread of life. Whoever comes
to me will never be hungry. Whoever
believes in me will not be thirsty.
—John 6:35

BY THE TIME I WAS in high school, I had been abused at home for years. My art ability qualified my enrollment into the commercial art program at York County Area Vocational Technical High School. This school was designed to equip students with trade skills to help them find entry-level jobs in their respective career fields when they graduate. I met my commercial art instructor. She sensed things were not right at home for me, and she also noticed incredible skills for my age at the time. She encouraged me and told me I was one of her favorite students. She seemed like a superhero to me because she understood what life was like for me. I excelled in art class. She nominated me for a National Art Award for black-and-white illustration and groomed me to compete in art competitions. She coordinated freelance art jobs for me to do on the weekends for her contacts in the industry. It was in her art class that my first girlfriend took a romantic interest in me.

I had one good friend in school. Joe was a tall, slender nursing student at the vocational technical high school. He suffered from diabetes, and he needed his insulin shot each day. His sense of humor was dry, like mine. I met him on the school bus. I was a new bus rider when I transferred to our school, and I was immediately a target for the bullies who sat in the rear of the bus simply because I kept quiet and to myself. Joe was a year older, and he instantly stood up to defend me. The bullies on the bus never bothered me again, thanks to Joe. I drew pictures for him to show my appreciation. He was willing to listen to me and understand what I was going through at home. Joe's father was a disabled veteran of the Army. My girlfriend was a year older, and she was acquainted with Joe from sharing a class with him. Our first dating experience was corrupted by the many years of sexual abuse I encountered beforehand. I had no idea what courtship was and thought dating was explicitly about sex. Of course, I was wrong. Within a few months of seeing me, she became pregnant, and a new challenge would face me as a teenage parent.

My life changed forever when my best friend Joe invited me to attend church with him at Bethany Baptist Church a month before my son was born in 1991. I was sixteen years old when I accepted Jesus Christ and received my very first Holy Bible from Ms. Irene at the church. Her advice to me as a new father is that every life is precious and that I should do the best I can and that parents can find comfort and guidance in the teachings of Jesus Christ. I wanted to provide a better life for him than mine. I did not want to be the same kind of parent as mine was, and I wanted to make his life better.

I was no longer just a student in school. I was a new father, and I began wondering more seriously how I could use my skills as an artist to provide for my son. My English teacher was sensitive to my situation at home and assigned me the role of Hamlet for the drama class play during my senior year. Learning about William Shakespeare and about Hamlet's tragic story helped to shape the lens through which I saw my own situation. I was an awkward introvert socially and had much in common with the character Hamlet. I could be bound in a nutshell and count myself king of an infinite space as I focused on my artwork and tasks at hand. Polonius' travel advice to his son Laertes would serve me well in the adventure to come.

Our families helped tremendously at first. I was seventeen when I graduated high school in 1992 and started looking for any work I could find. I realized just how scarce jobs were in a rural area, especially as a commercial artist, and so I worked as a dishwasher for the only restaurant in the town. My mother's husband, Charlie, passed away from lung cancer, and I moved back in with her now that her house was safer and free of domestic violence. She would end up being married a total of six times, but none of her other husbands were violent drunks. She used a portion of Charlie's life insurance money to pay tuition for me to attend a formal art school to increase my chances of finding work as an artist. I enrolled at Bradley Academy for the Visual Arts in York, Pennsylvania. It was a major blessing because I was the first person in my family to go to college of any kind. I earned an associate degree in specialized technology with a major in graphic design when I graduated in 1994.

I spent approximately four months looking for work, and it was just as hard as before to land a position as a young artist. Graphic design jobs were more likely to be found far away from home in larger cities. I understood what the phrase "starving artist" meant. It was a new challenge in life. Finally, I was hired to be a staff illustrator for a small printing company about an hour away from home in Mechanicsburg, PA. The drawing room was sheathed in wood paneling, and the only window was looking out into the vast indoor space where the printing presses were. Cigarette smoke filled the air. Two young ladies were already working there as staff artists. The art director was a woman with little creative vision, and she guarded the art supply room door with her desk parked in front of it. She questioned the need to withdraw every sheet of paper and tube of paint as if I planned to steal the expensive materials or use them for personal use.

I trudged along my commute each day. The cost of gas ate up most of my paycheck, and I needed a better job to take care of my son. I was dependent on my mother's help, and I did not like it. I wanted desperately to be independent and able to provide for my son. I was nineteen years old, and I would be twenty soon. I knew I needed something more. I didn't realize it at the time, but looking back now, I can see that God was listening to my prayers as his plans for me unfolded. I had no idea that I was about to leave home and embark on the adventure of a lifetime!

One day, during my commute to work, I saw an armed forces recruiting station. I felt a sense of urgency, so I stopped in to meet with the recruiters. They educated me about the military benefits of a steady paycheck, which was much better than what I was making at the time, and about the healthcare I could receive for my son. The only downside was that I would be away from home, but I could get thirty days of paid vacation each year to come home. I was instantly interested. I was impressed by the professional appearance of the recruiters in their uniforms. It brought back childhood memories of seeing service members march proudly in Armed Forces Day and Independence Day parades. I could imagine what it would be like to wear a uniform and be like one of them. I felt that a job in the military would be something to be proud of, but I was unaware of what the total cost would be in the end.

CHAPTER 3

ANSWERING
THE CALL

Trust in the LORD with all thine
heart; and lean not unto thine own
understanding. In all thy ways acknowledge
Him, and He shall direct thy paths.
—Proverbs 3:5–6

THE ARMY RECRUITER TOLD ME about a military occupational specialty titled Graphic Layout Specialist. The sergeant said that the Army has a school to attend for this specialty code immediately after finishing basic training. The only problem was that there was a waiting list for this school, and it would be over a year before I could leave home to join the Army. The Navy recruiter said that the Navy had a job rating titled Illustrator Draftsman. The Chief said that the Navy does not have a school for this job specialty because they depend on the recruit having already had formal art training before joining the Navy as a prerequisite. That suited me fine since I already had an associate degree in graphic design.

13

The Chief said that since there is no school for the illustrator draftsman job rating, I could ship out right away for Navy basic training. I could leave within a week! The only catch, of course, there was a catch, was that I would have to join the Navy with a general duty job code titled Seaman and perform the arduous duties of a Seaman until I became selected to be an Illustrator Draftsman through a competitive portfolio review after I was in the Navy. The Navy portfolio review happened once a year in Washington, DC, and I would have to wait about a year before I could submit my portfolio. It was a risk I weighed carefully in my mind.

I was determined to join the military because I felt the calling to serve something more important than just doing a job. I knew that I could get money for college and opportunities to travel. I realized that my chances of travel were greater if I joined the Navy. The romance and adventure of being a sailor on a ship at sea were appealing. I had never really been anywhere other than my hometown and local county. My current job and any local job I could possibly find could not compete with the long list of benefits of serving in the military.

Was I really willing to do any kind of dirty and hard work required of being a seaman? I knew my portfolio would be selected if I was only given a chance to submit one. I felt a rush of independence from being able to leave home and prove to my family that I was worth more than the rumors of being a deadbeat dad. I had made up my mind. I would join the Navy and perform the duties of a seaman until such a time as I could submit my portfolio and request to apply for the illustrator draftsman rating. I would finally leave home and be out on my own starting as soon as next week.

I signed the enlistment contract and proudly took the paperwork home. By this time, my mom was married to her sixth husband. Marvin was lucky number six. They would stay married for the next thirty years. He was also a career Army National Guard sergeant, so I just knew she would approve of my decision to join the military. I was wrong. The day I came home with my enlistment papers and showed them to my mom was a traumatic day. My mother was already under the influence of alcohol by the time I got home. She seemed proud and happy at first, but when I told her I was leaving next week, she changed her demeanor. She told me I was going to die in the military and that she disowned me as her son. She threw things at me and told me to get out of her house.

I called my older half sister. She let me stay with her for the next week at her house. I gave my job notice that I was joining the military. The response was mixed. My supervisor and boss called me into their office and asked if they could give me a pay raise to change my mind. I respectfully declined. The old lady at the front desk, who had worked there for so many years that I imagined her with her legs as tree roots under her desk, bid me farewell.

She said, "Follow your dreams, young man!"

That final week as a civilian passed quickly. My sister was proud to tell people her brother was joining the military. Most people said kind things in support of my decision. I let my sister cut my curly locks of hair since I knew I would have it cut in boot camp anyway. She shaved me bald, and it felt cold to feel the wind against the skin on my head. I looked like a new recruit. I was excited to leave. It was late November, and it was time to depart before I knew the week had passed. My half sister dropped me off with the recruiters, who took me to the train station in Harrisburg, Pennsylvania, along with two other new recruits.

I was placed in charge of the others because of my age. I was to make sure we made the train connections through to the Great Lakes north of Chicago, Illinois, where Navy basic training was located. This was the very first time traveling so far from home for me. The train ride would take over a day, so we shared a three-person sleeper car. It was nighttime and the shelves turned into beds as we each curled up, tired from a stressful day of leaving home. The train lurched forward, and I watched the landscape transform outside the window from suburban neighborhoods to rural farmland. Eventually, I saw snow blanketing the land, and the full moon illuminated the ground with an eerie glow.

Chicago was a stunning metropolis, far larger than each of our hometowns. The skyscrapers blocked out the sky, unlike anything I had seen before. Busy pedestrians and traffic zoomed by us as we stepped out from the train station to connect with a smaller train. The green double-decker train screeched to a halt before us on the upper platform. The digital sign displayed "Great Lakes," and we climbed aboard for the final leg of our journey. This was our last chance to enjoy the freedom of being a civilian. The train ride to boot camp was short. We entered the front gate of the base on a Sunday morning. The streets and barracks all seemed empty, and everything was so silent that a mouse could be heard. We didn't realize that it was a holiday routine on Sunday morning, and many of the recruits on base were attending church or ironing their uniforms. We were escorted to a cafeteria called a galley, where we were served lunch. Again, inside the galley, it was oddly quiet. There was no talking allowed. Only the scrapes of silverware could be heard throughout the enormous space. After we ate, we were escorted to a barracks building called Division Number Twelve. We were told to sit down by our bunk beds and wait in silence to meet our drill instructor, also known as a company commander. A red and white flag on the wall displayed "Company 091," and we could hear doors slamming in the distance as the flagpole seemed to shake and quiver.

In walked our drill instructor, looking immaculate in her dress uniform and taking precise steps. Many of us were surprised to see that our drill instructor was a woman. She called us to attention and walked past us, inspecting us. Her name was Petty Officer, First Class Christine Brown. She commanded the large room with her authority and stern countenance. I instantly feared her and knew I did not want to let her down. She explained the rules of the house and appointed various recruits to specific duties, such as the laundry petty officer to attend to our laundry bags and the religious studies petty officer to escort recruits to church on Sundays. Then the days became a blur of receiving inoculations and taking written tests based on the classes we attended. We trained in seamanship and firefighting, and we marched everywhere we went!

The marksmanship training was cancelled because the weapons range was closed for renovations. We were told that we would receive weapons training later on out in the fleet, if we ever actually needed it, because the Navy had its own security force. I had a hard time keeping up with the other recruits when we marched. I kept uttering under my breath, "Faith in God," with each footstep, hoping to be able to keep up. It was halfway through training when I fell behind. I got sick and fell way behind at the end of the fourth week! I was taking a written test and began to pass out as soon as I filled in my final answers. I fell to the floor, trying to breathe. I was drowning in fluids. Petty Officer Brown told another recruit to walk with me to the medical clinic, where I was diagnosed with double pneumonia.

The medics at the clinic had made a mistake. They pumped two intravenous bags of saline solution into me, assuming I was simply dehydrated. The doctor realized the mistake after the X-rays of my lungs were developed onto film. But now I was in serious danger of drowning because my body was diverting all fluids to my lungs because of the pneumonia. I was rushed off base in an ambulance and taken to the nearest hospital. The leading doctor of internal medicine greeted me and said I was about to be very sick, but that his staff was standing by for me. The next thing I can remember is being in bed surrounded by doctors who were shouting that they were losing me. I almost died.

I woke up in my hospital bed, dreading to hear bad news that I would be set back in training due to missing days of boot camp because of my illness. Christmas carols were playing on the television. The doctor and my drill instructor, Petty Officer Brown, walked in with grim looks on their faces. They asked me if there was anyone else they could contact at home besides my mother's phone number listed in my file. They said they called my mother last night because she was my next of kin, but she said she disowned me and to let me die.

I said, "I'm sorry; she was probably drunk when you tried calling her." I gave them my father's phone number. I didn't want to claim him as my next of kin because of the childhood sexual abuse. I felt particularly low as they stepped outside my room. I could hear the doctor and Petty Officer Brown arguing about whether or not to set me back a week in training because of my situation. My sweaty hands gripped the white hospital sheets in nervousness. The worst news for a recruit to hear is that they are being reassigned to another training division, meaning they will graduate later and be stuck in boot camp longer.

The doctor argued that I would need several weeks to recover from having had double pneumonia. Petty Officer Brown countered that she could catch me up on training I missed if I was released from the hospital in a few days. She is a tenacious woman. She won. I tried to get up out of my bed to stand at attention to address her and say thank you to her, but my diagnostic and oxygen connections were tangled up. She said, "Just relax; you are one of my best recruits. Get better; I'm going to have words with your family."

A couple of days passed as I was getting used to eating military hospital food and feeling well enough to stand up on my own. There was a knock at the door, and I was surprised to see my Uncle Russ standing there. Uncle Russ was one of the only successful members of our family. He enlisted in the US Air Force during the Vietnam War. He went on to climb the enlisted ranks to achieve the title of Senior Master Sergeant and retired from the military as a RADAR and microwave energy technician. He was working on completing his second career, installing microwave equipment in airlines. Everyone said that I should try to be like Uncle Russ when I grew up because he had his act together, and now here he was in person. I hadn't seen him since early childhood, during a family reunion, when he astonished us with his tales of living in Tokyo, Japan, for most of his military career.

He was a very tall and broad man with a deep, surly voice and a gray, curly beard. His presence was intimidating. "Your father couldn't come to visit you, so here I am!" he said. He brought me gifts. He gave me an ice-cold bottle of Coke and a set of markers with some drawing paper. He stayed with me all day long. He told long stories about his own experiences with basic training. He encouraged me and said that he knew I would become an officer one day. I drew him a thank-you note featuring people and equipment from each branch of the armed forces. He said he would cherish the artwork on his refrigerator at home.

The time had come for my discharge from the hospital and return to my own bunk bed back at the division. I thanked Petty

Officer Brown for helping me get back to her division and for letting me keep the art marker set my Uncle Russ gave me. She pulled me aside and said, "Look, I know it is going to be hard for you because you are still sick, and breathing is hard for you. Just try to do your best. Unfortunately, the final physical fitness test is coming up in a few days, and you will have to pass the test in order to graduate with my division."

I felt a new sense of dread. I barely passed the initial physical fitness test when I arrived at basic training. The test consisted of performing at least sixty curl-ups and sixty push-ups, followed by a mile-and-a-half run in under twelve minutes. The next two days flew by in the blink of an eye, and I was still struggling just to keep up and stay in step with the other recruits during normal marching at a brisk walking pace. Breathing the cold winter air hurt me like daggers in my lungs. It was now time to take the test.

I prayed to God as I struggled to breathe while running around the track for my final physical fitness test. To my surprise, Petty Officer Brown, dressed in her ceremonial blue uniform, rose from the table where the drill instructors watched and ran with me to help me keep the pace. I was thinking *"Faith in God"* with every breath and footfall as I concentrated on following her dress shoes. Finally, I just barely passed to move on and graduate on time with my division.

Sickness had more in store for me because when I received my graduation haircut, the barber noticed unusual bumps on my head. He sent me to medical, where I was diagnosed with chicken pox, which I never had as a child. I was returned to recover in isolation, away from other recruits, to the same internal medicine department at the hospital where I almost died earlier from pneumonia. I had the marker set and sketch pad my uncle gave me to pass the time in the hospital bed. I created thank-you cards for the doctors and nurses who were pleased but shocked to see me back with them so soon again.

After the graduation ceremony, I was granted weekend liberty and then left to see my family for two weeks before shipping off for my first duty station. Unlike the other recruits who gained muscle and looked fit and heroic in their dress blue uniforms, I was a skeleton at one hundred twenty-nine pounds with chicken pox marks all over my skinny and frail frame. I took a taxi from the base and went to the local shopping mall during my liberty time to see a movie. I was proud to be newly graduated and shocked when three men walked by and one of them spit on my uniform. I went to the bathroom to clean it up. I knew that they wanted to start a fight. I shook my head. Bullies always seem to try to bring others down, but I knew God was with me, and it was now my job to die if necessary to protect the rights of everyone in the country, including rude, ignorant people too. I was answering a higher calling.

Going home on leave was as much an adventure as leaving to go to basic training. It was the first time I ever flew on a plane. I met my family at Baltimore International Airport. My blue dress uniform drooped on me like a dress, and my family felt sorry for my skinny and scarred appearance. I was still recovering from double pneumonia. My mother quickly said, "I told you so," and "I knew this would happen," to all our relatives and her friends. My hometown felt slightly smaller than before, and I was eager to get away from it and report for duty to get on with my life in the Navy.

When my very first paycheck failed to manifest on payday, I discovered that I had a negative pay balance because my son's mother went to the county courthouse while I was away at basic training. Despite the allotment for support for her I made at the beginning of boot camp, my paycheck was further garnished for the entire amount of my son's birth three years ago, along with calculated "back support" for each month. The many checks I had written my son's mother were deemed "a gift" from me by the courthouse and not admissible as true child support because I gave her that money without an official order for support. I would not be paid a cent for my work in the US Navy until that balance was satisfied, which took eight months. During that time, I ate solely at the galley and stayed on base to shine my shoes after work in my barracks room. Again, my mother told me, "I told you so."

I was assigned to a dry dock for my first set of orders at a submarine base in Groton, Connecticut. One of the first supervisors I met was Petty Officer Souza. She reminded me of my drill instructor. She made me feel cared for by making numerous phone calls to resolve my pay problem. I remember she referred to me as "my sailor" on the telephone with others. I wanted to be like her one day and take care of my subordinates with the same zeal. Like another angel in my life, she was another positive role model to leave a lasting impression.

The dry dock stood six stories above the pier when it was in its up position, shaped like a giant napkin holder with a submarine inside resting on large blocks of wood. Down in the dirty, wet well of the dry dock, I worked as a member of the Deck department, where all the newly assigned seamen were sent. I swabbed and swept out the muck, hosed away the sea slime, and scraped barnacles from the hulls of submarines lifted out of the water for maintenance by the mighty dry dock.

One day, my supervising petty officer gathered three of us new recruits from the barracks and took us down to the piers of the lower submarine base, where the towering dry dock was. He asked for a volunteer to carry something, and the other two recruits quickly took steps backward, making me the volunteer. There I was, the skinniest and weakest recruit, trying to shoulder a heavy sack of floor tiles to carry up the precarious accommodation ladder to the top of the dry dock. I was praised for volunteering and for having a sharp-looking uniform. From that moment forward, I was never popular with the other deck sailors.

I took care of my uniform with pride to make it always inspection-ready, no matter how dirty the day's work soiled it. The other seamen stomped on the toes of my boots to smear away the shine I achieved to spite me. The best way to deal with bullies is to outshine them with better values and set a higher standard of performance. My chain of command noticed my efforts. The leading chief petty officer of the Deck department asked me what job I wanted to train for. I told him I wanted to be a Navy Illustrator Draftsman because I was an artist. He bellowed out in laughter and said, "You like to paint, do you? Well, I got a submarine out there that needs lots of paint on it!" Everyone laughed but me.

The days passed that way while I took each opportunity to work on my artwork on my bed in my barracks room. The US Navy held an annual portfolio review for those seeking to recode their job specialty to the coveted Illustrator Draftsman rating. In 1995, the Navy only had one hundred-two total illustrators in the whole service. Only one or two new illustrators were chosen each year. One foggy morning at work, I was in the garage of the Deck Department down on the pier. I froze in terror when I heard the commanding officer screaming my name in the front office. "Where is this, Seaman Addison?" he raged.

I felt like I was in trouble, but I did not know why. I forced my body forward to meet him at the position of attention. He looked at me with a big smile and made an announcement I will never forget. "From here on out, Seaman Addison is no longer assigned to the Deck Department, but he will report directly to me as our new command artist!" The commanding officer had recently reviewed my artwork as a requirement to certify that the work was my own. "Report to my office tomorrow morning!" he shouted.

Everyone was scared of the commanding officer, Lieutenant Commander Robert Archer. He smoked constantly and only gave mean responses to salutes and greetings. He held public captain's masts where sailors were punished and demoted for their misdeeds. He demanded the department heads report early and often on the status of their divisions. He drove a black sports utility vehicle parked at the very edge of the pier in his designated spot next to the dry dock. He was previously enlisted and was a strong leader.

I called home to tell the good news to my family, but I was so scared to see him personally face-to-face the next day. The next morning came swiftly, and I knocked on the commanding officer's door, but there was no answer. I realized I had arrived so early that even the boss was not there yet. My knees were weak, and my legs were trembling. I could hear him coming closer. He emerged through the hatch in the passageway and handed me his keys to open his office door. To my surprise, he greeted me with a warm smile and gave me a tour of his expansive office space, complete with a living room, a briefing room, and, of course, his mighty large desk. He said, "Seaman Addison, you will sit yourself at the end of the briefing table, and that will serve as your desk." Next, he ordered the supply officer to provide me with the art materials I would need to do a large illustration.

Commander Archer explained to me that he wanted me to do an illustration of the entire lower base and surrounding land, complete with the dry dock servicing a submarine featured prominently in the center. A few weeks passed as I toiled with my technical ink pen to create fine details like he wanted. I even showed little sailors, small as ants, working throughout the base and on the dry dock.

Each day as I worked, Commander Archer talked to me about leadership. He had me take books about being a successful Navy officer to my barracks to study at night. The next day, he would ask me what I thought about the readings or what I thought about a conversation he just had with other officers. I didn't realize that he was grooming me for leadership as an officer one day. I finished the illustration, my first official Navy drawing, in pen and ink with the perspectives I learned in art school. Next, he had me complete the top in calligraphy with the base commodore's name.

The supply officer framed the work of art, and Commander Archer said, "Seaman Addison, you are about to see how things work." He donned his hat and jacket, and we left to go to the base headquarters. With the confidence of a hero, he opened the door to a conference room and interrupted the commodore's briefing to the senior officers on the base. Commander Archer said, "Excuse us, commodore, but Seaman Addison has taken it upon himself to produce this illustration of the Navy at work here, and we are here to present this amazing gift to you." I was surprised. I had no idea that I was actually making the illustration for the commodore. The commodore was grateful, and his executive assistant took a photo while he gave a short speech demonstrating his thanks. We were about to leave and exit the conference room door when Commander Archer turned back and said, "Oh, commodore, one last thing: Seaman Addison's portfolio is being reviewed right now by the selection board in Washington, DC. He would very much like to be an illustrator draftsman for the United States Navy, and anything you can do would be appreciated."

The commodore said, "I will make a phone call today."

A few days later, the phone rang on Commander Archer's desk. It was the senior selection board member calling to tell my chain of command that I had been selected as an Illustrator Draftsman and that I would receive orders to a nice location for my next job in the Navy. I received orders to be stationed in Denmark to work for the North Atlantic Treaty Organization (NATO). I was to receive weapons training and qualify with a rifle and pistol before reporting for duty, but the base security officer said that such training opportunities were limited to his security staff. "Don't worry," he said, "You will get the weapons training overseas at your next duty station, if you really need it."

CHAPTER 4

FAR AND AWAY

For I know the plans I have for you, declares the
LORD, plans to prosper you and not to harm
you, plans to give you a hope and a future.
—Jeremiah 29:11

I DIDN'T KNOW THAT DENMARK was a country when the assignment officer told me that was where I was going. I asked, "Was I going to be on a ship named USS Denmark?" He laughed at me over the phone and told me it was a country in northern Europe where the Vikings came from. I went to the base library and began studying about Danish culture, land, and people. I obtained my passport and a small Danish language dictionary. I packed my bags and left for an even larger adventure, even further away from home.

It was 1996, and my first eight-hour trip across the Atlantic Ocean on a British Airways plane was too exciting to sleep. The flight attendants were kind, and they took the time to talk to me about my destination. I learned about the long daylight hours of the summer months and equally long dark winter nights there. After a brief lay-over in London, I arrived in Copenhagen and took a smaller flight to Karup, Denmark. The US military has a sponsor program where an experienced person is assigned to meet and greet new arrivals and help them get settled in.

My sponsor drove me to a hotel room where I would be living temporarily until an apartment called a "flat" was available for me to live in. There were no barracks rooms for the small contingent of American soldiers at the base where the NATO peace headquarters was located. A contracted bus ran a route through town to take us to work each day. My hotel room was extravagant. It featured a kitchen, bedroom, and multiple shower nozzles. I felt like a prince living in a fairy tale. I dreamed of seeing Europe one day, but I could never have traveled like this if it wasn't for the military. I couldn't believe that I would actually be living and working as an artist there for three years.

My excitement faded on my first day at the base, where I learned exactly what type of work I would be doing. I was assigned to work in what was called the reprographics room at the headquarters. It was a room full of photocopy machines. My chain of command explained to me that they had been working just fine without an American illustrator on the staff since the last one departed several months ago. Besides, there were two very competent German soldiers working in the drawing room, where there was barely enough illustration work to keep them busy.

A lesson I would learn well during my time in the military is that you work where you are needed, not where you prefer to. The whole of the unit's mission is greater than the wants of a single individual. After cleaning toilets and scraping barnacles at my previous duty station, this was still a dream job to be in a climate-controlled office space. I set about immediately studying the operator's manuals of all the machines and paper binding equipment under my charge. I took ownership of the room with a sense of pride and cleaned places that had been long neglected. The office shined. My customers were the many staff officers of the multinational team, ranging from privates to general officers. I focused on the efficient delivery of stacks of print requests and exceeding customer expectations.

The next year passed quickly. My apartment was on the ground floor, adjacent to cobblestone walking streets designated for pedestrians only, where the townspeople shopped for what they needed on a day-to-day basis. In the evenings and on weekends, I was free to explore Denmark by bus and rail. The trains were remarkably clean and safe for a solo traveler. It is a beautiful landscape with a very low crime rate. Denmark is home to the amusement attraction Lego Land, and the famous Little Mermaid statue can be spotted in Copenhagen. To the north of Copenhagen, visitors can tour Elsinore Castle. It served as the inspiration for the setting of William Shakespeare's play Hamlet.

Once a month, I performed courier duties, carrying documents to NATO bases in Germany. During one trip, my escort took me to visit the Bergen-Belsen memorial, where thousands of former concentration camp victims perished. I vividly recall several large mounds above the ground marked with stones simply etched with a number, such as fifteen thousand, indicating how many bodies lay below. The terrible holocaust must never be forgotten. I wish everyone could feel the sadness that physically walking such a site brings. The visitor center was very educational and respectfully somber as spectators silently proceeded through the gallery of exhibits.

My adventure in Europe matured me and educated me in ways that attending college could not. The high rate of speed from driving on the German highway called the Autobahn was thrilling and made me appreciate safe driving. European driver's licenses are expensive and more difficult to acquire than in the United States. There was a white circle sign with four black diagonal lines that signaled the end of all restrictions. Our government sedan sank low to hug the road at increased speeds. Beautiful mountains with quaint villages and industrialized cities zoomed by.

I sent souvenirs home, including every chance I got, but they were a poor substitute for my actually being there. I paid for calling cards to make long-distance phone calls to loved ones.

Email was relatively new, but old-fashioned letters were always welcome reading. I could tell that my mother's hard feelings about me joining the military were softening, and she was increasingly proud to speak of her son's service with her coworkers. I came to realize that she simply missed me very much, and she wished I had never left home to begin with. She loved hearing about my visit to London for a week, where I explored the Tower of London, walked across the Tower Bridge, and enjoyed a double-decker bus ride through Piccadilly Circus. I saw my first live plays performed in a theater. The Phantom of the Opera and Cyrano de Bergerac are experiences I will always cherish. I was gaining an education that can't be had in traditional classrooms.

I was still somewhat embarrassed by the fact that I merely made photocopies for the headquarters. My ego and selfish desire to be employed as the artist that I was designated to be occupied my thoughts. I knew deep down that I was capable of doing more than I was. A British Sergeant Major visited me to see how I was doing, and he listened as I vented my frustrations. His advice was that I should take time to read the official correspondence that was intended for the troops instead of merely taking the print request and copying the document. He said that this would give me more situational awareness about what was going on at work, and I would feel more valued as a team member. He was right.

I had so much to learn about military staffing, strategy, policy, and procedures. I was at a staff dinner where I met a senior German Navy commander. He revealed that he was an accomplished artist. He presented a beautifully framed painting of a battleship to the admiral at the end of the dinner. He told me he was aware of my talents, and he knew about my frustration at work making photocopies instead of filling the vacant illustrator post in the drawing room. He said that the joy of creating art should not be limited to what the task at hand is. He reminded me that I was always free, like him, to create artwork during my free time at home, just as he did.

It opened my eyes and made me ask myself: What was the purpose of doing art? Was I doing it for my own glory or to share the beauty of God's creation with others? It finally dawned on me that it was more important to be a valued military team member than it was to shine as an individual. I realized art was a gift meant to be shared, so I started making gift illustrations for the other American families stationed there. I was invited to teach art to the British and American students at the international school, and I designed and helped paint the background set for their annual school Christmas play. Art opened doors for me, but it was up to me to have faith and follow where the path beyond led.

It was 1997 when I noticed that volunteers were needed to deploy as members of the joint-service multinational peacekeeping force to the former Yugoslavia. I had not deployed yet, and I was excited at the opportunity to deploy. I approached the senior US military officer present at the headquarters, a US Marine Corps colonel, and he cautioned me before saying yes. "I have no doubt you will represent us well, Ben, but be careful of what you wish for." Orders were issued for me to draw equipment and weapons from the supply department, attend training, and report to the NATO-led Stabilization Force Headquarters in Zagreb, Croatia.

"*Hmmm, weapons,*" I thought. "I hadn't had any weapons training yet." I raised the issue with my chain of command and was told that marksmanship training was reserved for the Danish Army soldiers since they were the ones charged with the defense of the headquarters, and besides, they had no American weapons there to issue me. I was told that I would stop at a NATO base in Naples, Italy, to receive my gear, and I would likely receive any necessary weapons training there shortly before I reported for duty in the combat zone. Trusting this, I proceeded to fly to Rome and then to Naples. There was no sponsor to escort me, so I found my way to the barracks and checked into temporary lodging. I asked around and found out that the only training offered at the base was a mine warfare awareness class since Bosnia-Herzegovina, Croatia, and Serbia were littered with land mines.

Incoming personnel had to know how to recognize and avoid potential booby traps. As far as weapons training went, I was asked why I hadn't already received the required training and familiarization. US Navy personnel did not often deploy into this theater of operations, and US Army personnel brought their weapons with them from the United States. A decision was made to have the US Air Force security garrison at the airport quickly train me and issue me weapons. The training officer was annoyed that he had to train me. He reached around me to adjust my pistol grip and practically squeezed the trigger himself, firing off a few rounds. He ejected the magazine, which held the remaining bullets, and handed it to me. The Airman said, "There you go. You're qualified. Come sign for your weapons."

I nervously returned to my barracks room and waited for my flight to Sarajevo the next morning. The next morning, I boarded a cargo plane full of soldiers bound for the former Yugoslavia. I clumsily took a vacant spot in the cargo net seating, and the more experienced soldiers seated on either side of me began correcting discrepancies in my uniform and weapons conditions. It was a moment of big brothers taking care of a younger brother that I will never forget. I felt like I had angels looking out for me. The buildings in Sarajevo were all damaged and riddled with bullet holes. It was my first time seeing a war zone in person.

A local taxi driver approached me and begged me to take his young daughter home to the United States and marry her. He wanted a better life for her, and I gained a new perspective about what a privilege it is to be an American. Home looks different after you travel. My ambition to be employed as an artist was insignificant in comparison to this man's desire for his child. I apologized to the man and said that I was afraid I couldn't accept his offer. He pleaded his case one more time before being told to leave the camp perimeter by another soldier. I felt sorry for him. I actually considered the possibility of doing it just to save one life from poverty, but what did I know about marriage? I was only twenty-two years old.

I traveled north to my post and saw firsthand the ravages of war. Not only were buildings and monuments destroyed, but so were people's lives. Fertile farmland was now off-limits because it had been seeded with antitank and antipersonnel land mines. The orange and red international triangular signs with a black skull and crossbones symbols warned of mines. My general administrative duties at the Stabilization Force Support Headquarters included being a courier for international correspondence. Each day, my Air Force partner and I loaded bags of mail and delivered them to camps at the heavily mined airport. It was a dangerous route to take in an unarmored vehicle. At times, we drove just feet away from the border of overgrown fields where the mines were. Sometimes the mines would detonate, and we would take cover. Radio frequencies, animals, and weather conditions could set them off.

The highlight of our daily trip to the airport was a meager but meaningful lunch. We stopped at a woman's house for the sandwiches she made. They were poor excuses for a proper meal, sometimes consisting of just a scrap of bread and a piece of dried pepperoni, with maybe a leaf of lettuce. I learned that the point of buying her food was for charity. Soldiers dug deep into their pockets to compensate her for the meager food. Her daughter helped her in the kitchen. She had been reportedly raped during the ethnic cleansing that took place before NATO came to establish peace. Her missing front tooth was noticeable when she smiled. Her mother never stopped trying to get one of us to marry her. She would point to our names on our uniforms and say, "See here, they are Americans! He will make a good husband for you." The short, week-long pre-deployment training did not cover these situations. I felt bad and paid as much as I could afford for the woman's food offerings. I learned that I had a lot of freedoms and security to be thankful for and that my family situation wasn't as bad as others around the world.

The climax of my deployment came during a convoy to Sarajevo to act as a courier for urgent material. A special warfare security expert offered to drive three of us around Sarajevo to take photos. I had a small disposable cardboard camera, which was popular at the time. I sat in the back of his sedan alongside a Navy chaplain who was also interested in seeing the terrain more closely. While we were up on a ridge overlooking the decimated city, a radio call came across that said a riot was in progress downtown, and all units were to report back to base. The special warfare operator stopped the car at the top of the hill, where we could see demonstrators blocking the city streets. He told us to chamber a round into our pistols and make them ready for shooting. I fumbled with my pistol since I never had the proper training. The Navy Chaplain reached over and helped me. I was embarrassed and afraid. I was afraid of the potential of having to use a weapon I was unfamiliar with in a real-world situation. The protesters rocked the car and banged on the windows. They were angry and tired of living in poverty. The car bounced and rolled forward slowly so as not to hurt anyone. It felt like an eternity. I made a promise to myself that somehow I would get proper weapons handling training if I were to continue my Navy career.

At the end of my deployment, I met US Air Force Staff Sergeant Ken Barber, who was also a minister. He prayed with me, and he gave me a men's devotional Holy Bible. Ken reminded me that we are always brothers in faith and that everything happens according to God's bigger picture. We prayed for peace and guidance. I was grateful to have been a part of such an important mission. I knew that I grew from the experience. I was more appreciative of the things I took for granted.

Even though I wasn't assigned there to do artwork during my deployment, I produced illustrations of the headquarters compound and of the flags of the participating allied peacekeeping countries for the commanding general. He awarded me an engraved commander's coin as a token of his appreciation for a job well done. As I thought about the bigger picture, I began to realize that I was grateful to learn and grow as a service member and satisfied that I was able to do my artwork in my free time.

I returned to my parent NATO headquarters in Denmark, and I was very happy to hear some good news. A position in the drawing room finally opened up for me. Word that I was an illustrator spread while I was away, and before I knew it, I was being asked to design logos, t-shirts, coins, and hats and create illustrations of the headquarters building for the Admiral's office. I was thrilled the day my commander reassigned me down the hall to the drawing office. My supervisor was a German Army Master Sergeant, and he taught me the art of photography and darkroom wet film development. I became the command's official photographer in addition to my duties in graphic design.

That year flew by. I loved my job, and I was able to visit Norway, Sweden, Germany, Luxemburg, the Netherlands, the United Kingdom, Belgium, and Austria. Denmark was my favorite because being stationed there felt like a second home, and I loved the history of the Vikings. I just happened to have a very light complexion with sandy blonde hair and blue eyes, so I not only lived in Denmark, but locals thought I was actually Danish! I took it as a compliment. My tour overseas helped me grow in ways I could never have imagined. I was promoted to Petty Officer Second Class and earned two Joint Service Commendation Medals. I learned to see the United States from the point of view of other countries, and I gained a deeper sense of appreciation for what it means to be an American. Before I knew it, my enlistment was up, and I had to make a major decision. It was time to decide whether to reenlist or go home.

CHAPTER 5

HITTING THE TARGET

As every man hath received the gift, even so
minister the same one to another, as good
stewards of the manifold grace of God.
—1 Peter 4:10

THE DECISION TO REENLIST IS a heavy decision for every service member. You have to weigh the benefits of service against the sacrifices made. My service overseas was already very costly in terms of hurting my relationships with family members. It was prohibitively expensive to fly home on leave, so I was only able to fly home once during my three-year tour in Europe. When I did come home, the two weeks of vacation time flew by in the blink of an eye. Military family members also sacrifice for your service by carrying on with life and not having you around.

The pain of missed birthdays, marriages, and anniversaries stung sharply. I knew that my son was growing closer to his stepfather than me because of my absence. I learned to accept that because I was providing a level of health care and financial stability for him that I couldn't otherwise provide if it wasn't for my service in the military. The benefits for military dependents are substantial. Ultimately, I opted to reenlist. After renewing my oath and signing my contract, it was time to talk to my assignment officer to find out where my next set of orders would send me. I hoped to continue working as a military artist or photographer as I had at the end of my job at the NATO headquarters. I braced for the bad news.

The assignment officer said that the Navy was doing away with its illustrator positions, and unfortunately, he had nowhere to send me that I could actually do artists' work. I was due for sea duty, so he stashed me in a fleet of F-18 squadrons of fighter jets based at the Master Jet Base at Naval Air Station Oceana in Virginia. I would fill a general duty billet, which meant that I would be tasked to do any odd jobs they needed me to do. The only bright side was that my next duty station was a drivable distance from my hometown, and I could visit with my family more often when I had leave and on long weekends. In March of 1999, I reported to the hangar of Fighter Squadron *one three one*. The command's Master Chief Petty Officer assigned me to their operations department, where I would deal with communications traffic and assist the pilots with tracking fight schedules. I was out of my comfort zone, but by now I had learned to take ownership of any job and do my best at it. What it meant to serve changed for me over time. Instead of serving just as an artist, I was serving as a leader. I wanted to make a difference in the world. I became the supervising petty officer of a small group of sailors, and I was promoted to petty officer first class.

The naval aviators in the squadron were impressive officers. The ones in my chain of command were genuinely interested in my professional development, and I remember a piece of advice one of them gave me that was as clear as if it were just yesterday. US Air Force Exchange Officer Major Doty told me one day that he was impressed with the quality of my work, but I should try to see the bigger picture. I began to contemplate the larger strategic effects of our deployment in a post-Cold War era. Suddenly, my sense of purpose felt more satisfied. I could learn to accept that I might be an artist in title only, and the only artwork I was doing was collateral assignments to design commemorative items with the squadron's logo. My work in squadron operations helped me realize my role in a bigger world. It was still important to remember the lessons of basic training. Following instructions, paying attention to detail, showing up early, exceeding expectations, and working hard contributed to my successful rise up the enlisted ranks faster than my peers.

I shared my story about never having had proper marksmanship training and ending up needing that skill in a real-world situation in Sarajevo. The training officer said, "I'm sorry, but training opportunities are limited to the pilots only, since they are likely the only ones in the squadron to potentially be shot down and need to use their sidearm. I was frustrated at the class divide between the officers and the enlisted ranks. As an enlisted sailor, my job was to keep the ready room and hangar office spaces clean at all times and clean up the bathrooms as well. One day, a pilot's "piddle pack" urine bag was left improperly disposed of in the regular waste receptacle, and it exploded, causing a tremendous mess. It was severely humbling to be a noncommissioned officer reduced to menial janitorial duties. These duties were especially disheartening aboard ship when we joined with an aircraft carrier's crew for deployment across the ocean.

The squadron and its maintenance personnel travel often between air stations and the ship during what are called "work-up trips" before committing to the long deployment. The various locations provide valuable training opportunities. We were on temporary duty at Naval Air Station Fallon in Nevada when my department head revealed a surprise for me. He heard about my desire to learn to handle weapons and about my story in the former Yugoslavia, and kept me in mind when making arrangements for the squadron's exercises. One of the tests of the pilots is to communicate with a ground element of soldiers to simulate providing combat support for troops on the ground.

Navy special sea, air, and land warfare operators (Navy SEALs) used this opportunity to gain target practice with all their weapons to create realistic background noises for the pilot to have to listen through over the radio when talking to the ground. I was invited to spend the day at the range with the SEALs and get familiar with each of the weapons they brought. They taught me the importance of breathing control, trigger squeezing, and follow-through. By the end of the day, I was fairly comfortable using the weapons, even though I hoped I would never actually need them again as a military artist. I was very appreciative of the squadron pilots for providing me with that educational experience. I returned to the hangar with my uniform covered in desert dust and smelling like gunpowder. I did not know that this training would eventually serve a greater purpose later on during my time in the Navy.

Our squadron began work-ups for deployment onboard the Nimitz-class nuclear-powered aircraft carrier USS Dwight D. Eisenhower. Our short trips at sea grew longer as training intensified. We enjoyed a port visit at St. Thomas in the Virgin Islands. I never imagined I would be in such a tropical paradise. The flavor of coconut, the scent of clean sea spray, and the warmth of the sun relaxed me. I took part in a scuba diving excursion. We dove fifty feet deep in crystal-clear waters. The sensation felt like flying.

We deployed in February 2000. Crossing the Atlantic Ocean was a life-changing experience. Imagine looking in every direction into the horizon only to see the white caps of waves. Occasionally, we would see a group of dolphins jumping out of the water in a long line formation adjacent to the mighty warship's wake. Life on an aircraft carrier is like living in a crowded city with every imaginable service available for the crew, including a barber shop, a ship's store, multiple galleys, and medical services. The food is plentiful, with lots of variety to choose from. Breakfast was my favorite because I could have scrambled eggs and orange juice. A midnight meal served as a second lunch for the sailors working night shifts.

The scent of jet fuel permeated the air, and the thunderous pounding of jets landing above our heads on the flight deck became routine background details. We took Navy showers to conserve potable water by turning the water off when lathering up with soap. I lived in a ninety-man berthing compartment with bunk beds stacked like shelves three high. The more senior petty officers picked the best beds. The sleeping quarters smelled like dirty socks and aftershave lotion. Hushed whispers, snoring, and sounds of lockers being opened and closed filled the maze-like room. Red lights were used to help eyes adjust to night vision for the night shift and to help sailors sleep. Days would easily pass at a stretch without seeing the sunshine outside the skin of the ship. In the huge hangar bays, the large open hangar bay doors were like theater stages, and the star of the show was the ocean's waves rushing by the ship. There were seagulls from home that nestled high up in the ceiling of the hangar, and sailors would feed them pieces of bread brought from the galley as if the birds were lucky mascots.

There is a media department on aircraft carriers where at least one Navy illustrator was sure to be found working on certificates and drawings among the ship's photographers. I sought him out while we were underway, and I introduced myself. We military artists rarely got to meet one another because we were far and few between. I was amazed that he actually got to do illustration work compared with all the difficulty I had with getting assigned such a post as his. I offered to help him with his work when my duties with the squadron permitted, but he politely declined. I felt downtrodden and remembered not to treat others that way if the roles were reversed.

During the deployment, we transited the Strait of Gibraltar and passed into the Mediterranean Sea. We made port visits throughout our journey. In Trieste, Italy, I took a train ride to Venice and walked along the famous romantic canals. In Dubrovnik, Croatia, I explored the castle-like fortress walls around the edge of the ancient city. In Corfu, Greece, I ate fresh seafood. In Souda Bay, Crete, I visited the archaeological site of Knossos. In Antalya, Turkey, I had hot tea and bought exquisite leather goods. In Haifa, Israel, I was given my cherished crucifix, which was handcrafted in Jerusalem. In Bahrain, I felt the desert heat, and in Jebel Ali, in the United Arab Emirates, I experienced the wealthy city of Dubai. In Lisbon, Portugal, I took a motor scooter tour of the city.

Many sailors find the first bar or restaurant that serves alcohol they come to when they leave the ship and stay there for the duration of their liberty. I preferred to take advantage of the tours and have more meaningful memories to share. At night, when it was time to return to the ship, long lines of sailors waited their turn to board the mighty aircraft carrier. Several had too much to drink and were carried back by their shipmates.

During the long days of performing my duties, I tried to see the bigger picture of the strategic importance of a carrier's deployment. I earned both my enlisted surface warfare and enlisted aviation warfare pins by demonstrating proficiency in various operations and tasks. I felt that I was capable of doing and being more in the Navy, so I expressed an interest in becoming an officer, but I didn't have a four-year college degree. My goals for joining the military were to provide for my family, to see the world, and to get money to go to college. The military's tuition assistance program pays for college classes you take on active duty. The trick is to find the time. My time was already stretched thin from volunteering to work extra shifts and studying to earn warfare qualifications.

The Navy has competitive programs for enlisted sailors to earn a four-year degree and a commission as an officer. I would need to study for the Scholastic Assessment Test (SAT). I was weak in the major subjects tested because, back when I was in school, the only subject that interested me was art. The pilots of Strike Fighter Squadron *one three one* came to my rescue again. They tutored me in math and English for four months during the deployment between their administrative duties when they weren't busy flying missions. I got to sit in their chairs in the ready room and pilot briefing rooms while I received lessons in algebra, geometry, and grammar. I ended up passing my SAT with a competitive score of one thousand two hundred forty! I wasn't selected for a commissioning program that year, but it was only my first application attempt. I remained determined that I wanted to elevate my status and the quality of life I could provide for my family, so I kept applying. I prayed for guidance and patience.

CHAPTER 6

LOVE AND WAR

A friend loves at all times, and a
brother is born for adversity.
—Proverbs 17:17

HOMECOMING FROM DEPLOYMENT IS A spectacle to behold on the pier as the aircraft carrier returns from deployment. A crowd of thousands of loved ones for the more than five thousand crew members floods the parking lot and looks to reunite with their sailor. Sailors lining the rails of the ship in their dress uniforms wave down at the crowd and look for banner signs with their name or a predetermined marker to help them find their family in the sea of people. A rush of emotion pulses with heavy heartbeats and flowing tears as loved ones embrace after months of separation. The good feelings continue as lifestyles return to normal.

Coming home makes you appreciate everything, from being with the people you love to certain foods again. Each time, home gets smaller and smaller because you see it from a much larger perspective of traveling the world. Some sailors come home to newly born babies, and new fathers are among the first in line to get to depart the ship. I was anxious to take leave and drive home to see my family. I missed my son, my siblings, my mother, and my best friend, Joe. Sailors earn thirty days of paid vacation time a year, and spending it is one of the sweetest sensations. My family updated me on all that I missed while I was away, and they eagerly listened to my stories about deployment. Back at work, the routine of preparing for the next deployment resumed. Small, short training trips were the order of the day.

In the spring of 2001, the squadron was in Key West, Florida, for predeployment training when I met my beautiful wife, Leandra. She was there on vacation with her friends, and I was enjoying my off-duty time in the popular tourist destination. Beaches and palm trees punctuated a picture-perfect romance. We were like kindred spirits who found each other in the world. She was like an angel to me. I remember explaining to her the hardships expected from being married to a sailor, but that didn't stop us from getting married just a few months later in the following summer. Shortly afterward, we found out we would be having a baby! My wife worked at a local department store, and her coworker Betty invited us over for dinner. Imagine my surprise to find out her husband was the executive officer of my very first duty station in Connecticut, and he remembered me! Jim and Betty became dear friends and part of our family. They looked out for my wife when I was away on the ship, just like a pair of guardian angels. We still keep in touch to this day.

A salty older sailor explained to me that every deployment is different, no matter how many you go on because your family conditions are different each time. Children are older, loved ones get married or divorced, and schools change. I was extremely proud to be a father again, and my wife took care of my son as if he were her own. She helped me press the court system to earn visitation rights. Now that she was part of my life, I could offer my son a more stable setting for him to visit me in the eyes of the court. I was away on a training detachment onboard the aircraft carrier USS John F. Kennedy in Mayport, Florida. My wife was in my hometown visiting my son and my side of the family when the news of an attack on the World Trade Center and Pentagon broke on the morning of September 11, 2001.

All military units were mobilized. We went to battle stations and cut the lines to the mighty warship to get her underway as quickly as possible. The air wing's fighter jets joined us and landed on deck as soon as we were on guard station just off the East Coast. All commercial flights were grounded, and we sailed up the coast to form a protective bubble of air space with our sensors and combat air patrols. As the dust settled from the attack, a new wave of patriotism swept across the country, and recruiting stations were swamped with eager candidates wanting to serve their country. The global war on terror began, and our target was the Taliban in Afghanistan. Our aircraft carrier and accompanying ships in our strike group rushed the final measures of pre-deployment training so that we could get on station. I volunteered to leave early for deployment, which was a difficult decision because Leandra was pregnant. My wife has always been strong and independent, so with the support of my chain of command and her coworkers behind her, I left.

The combat deployment was a different experience than the previous deployment. We sailed across the Atlantic Ocean and bypassed traditional port visits in the Mediterranean Sea in record time. Our transit through the Suez Canal was surreal. Vast desert landscapes lined each side of the narrow edges of the Suez, and the width of the aircraft carrier is so wide that from the flight deck, it looks like the ship is sailing through the yellow, blazing hot sands. Before we knew it, we were through the Red Sea, and on station in the Indian Ocean to launch airstrikes in support of military operations in Afghanistan.

My duties in operations required me to wake up before many of my shipmates, so I put my creativity to good use. Using dry-erase markers on a whiteboard on the wall in berthing, I drew daily cartoons about our situation to lighten the mood. The other petty officers said they looked forward to waking up to see what the new cartoon would be. Artists throughout the ship painted motivational murals on the ship's hatches and bulkheads depicting the heroic efforts of the first responders on September 11. I designed the door signs for all the squadron work centers with the Strike Fighter Squadron *one three one* Wildcat logo.

Instead of port visits, we were treated with what are called "beer days." On the seventieth consecutive day at sea, with no port visit in the foreseeable future due to the need to remain on station and conduct operations, two cans of beer were distributed to each sailor. The event, in hindsight, is sadly comical. The consumption of alcohol is forbidden on modern US Navy warships, so it was quite the spectacle to see pallets of cases of beer brought onboard during supply replenishments, and quickly, the beer was placed under armed guard until the inevitable day of distribution.

A beer day is a sad milestone for sailors because they would much prefer to relax in a foreign port. The ship takes a brief pause in operations and usually has what is called "a steel beach picnic," where hamburgers and hotdogs are cooked, music is played on the loudspeakers, and a ball is played on open areas of the flight deck. The food is a nice change of pace from meals made with chicken and rice. Sometimes, if conditions are right, a swim call is organized, and sailors with guns stand watch, looking out for sharks, while the others climb down the fantail at the rear of the ship to swim in the ocean. We had multiple beer days during that extended deployment. I didn't work as an artist much during that deployment, but I earned multiple Navy Achievement Medals for my performance and administrative accomplishments.

We sailed more than sixty thousand miles, logged 10,973 flight hours, and dropped sixty-four thousand pounds of ordnance on Taliban and al-Qaeda targets. I was proud to be a part of such an important mission. Most importantly, I was a proud new father. An American Red Cross message transmitted the details of my daughter's birth, and I carried that piece of paper in my pocket for the remaining three months of the deployment. I was a nervous wreck, and I couldn't concentrate on my duties until I knew that both my baby and my wife were doing well.

When we returned home, there they were. My wife and daughter were waiting on the pier for me to finally leave the ship and go home on leave with them. It was again time to decide whether or not to reenlist. The prohibitively high cost of civilian health care and the unlikelihood that I could find a job making as much as I was in the Navy drove my decision. It was obvious to me that I could best continue to provide for my family by staying in the Navy. I had high hopes that my work could finally match my job title of illustrator at my next duty station, but it was not to be. Once again, the assignment officer had grim news regarding the dwindling supply of illustrator positions left in the Navy. I was given a choice. I could go become a recruiter, or I could become a drill instructor at Navy basic training. For me, the choice was simple. I could never picture myself as a salesman or try to persuade the unwilling to join the military. I knew that the shore duty hours would be difficult and demanding, but my career would benefit from taking on the much more arduous duties of a drill instructor. We relocated to Great Lakes, Illinois, in October 2002, and I was back on old stomping grounds.

CHAPTER 7

SHAPING THE FUTURE

O my people, hear my teaching; listen to
the words of my mouth. What we have
heard and known, what our fathers have
told us. We will not hide them from their
children; we will tell the next generation
the praiseworthy deeds of the LORD, his
power, and the wonders he has done.
—Psalm 78

I COMPLETED INSTRUCTOR TRAINING AND started drill instructor training with a heavy heart. I felt the farthest from my original goal of being a Navy artist. Although I carried the official title of illustrator with my rank of paygrade E-6, I was, in fact, doing the job of a teacher. I tried to remember the advice that I could always do my artwork as a hobby at home and find comfort in that thought, but the truth is that I would have very little time at home with this new assignment. Drill instructors work long hours. I was to wake the recruits up in the morning and put them to bed at night. After I put the recruits to bed, they approached me for individual counseling. Many were simply homesick or unsure about the details of their enlistment contract. I often had to break bad news to recruits that their recruiters somehow neglected to mention.

My wife worked full time in retail, and our daughter was passed between three sets of childcare each day. Many days, we communicated through sticky notes left on the refrigerator door. "Buy milk" and "Don't forget your doctor's appointment" were some of the messages. I was quiet as a mouse when I came home after midnight and usually just rested downstairs in the recliner for a few hours before leaving to go back to work in time to wake up my recruits. It was simply bad timing to press my son's mother for visitation rights with my son. My wife and I took parenting classes offered by the Navy's Fleet and Family Support Center, and we provided statements from our neighbors in Navy family housing to demonstrate our suitability to have a visitation with my son for the legal system. We won the visitation thanks to my wife's persistence and an understanding judge. The only problem was that my son's first summer stay with us would coincide with the beginning of my very first division of recruits to train. Talk about bad timing! I struggled to make my son feel comfortable and loved while balancing work and a precious few off-duty hours.

The time had come to begin taking the test for advancement to Chief Petty Officer. Many sailors retire from their careers without obtaining the rank of Navy Chief. After passing the annual written examination, a selection board convenes to choose the best-qualified candidates, who then undergo an initiation period during the summer months. Despite passing the test for Chief Illustrator Draftsman for three years in a row, there were zero quotas available. This meant that no matter how good you scored, there was simply no vacancy to promote. At that time, there were only three authorized Navy Chief billets for Illustrators, and there were nine actual people at that rank. The Navy had overpromoted too many. I would have to wait until they left the service to open up a vacancy to promote.

During my first attempt at the chief's examination, I was seated in a room of candidates waiting for permission to begin the test when I saw a familiar face. It was the face of my original drill instructor, Petty Officer Dillsworth. She looked exactly the same as she did back in 1994, when she trained me. Her formidable and commanding presence distracted me from my test. Service members usually never forget their drill instructors because of the powerful impact they have. I timed turning my test in to match her doing the same, and I met her out in the hallway. I said, "Excuse me; I doubt you remember me, but you were my drill instructor from eight years ago, and I want to say thank you."

"I remember you," she said. "You got pneumonia and almost died, and then you got chicken pox just before graduating."

My jaw dropped open. "How many divisions of recruits have you trained?" I was surprised she remembered me among so many.

"More than thirty divisions," she replied. I immediately asked her to be my mentor as I completed drill instructor training. I was only beginning to follow in her footsteps. I confided in her, and she gave me sound advice. She genuinely cared about each and every recruit she trained. Good drill instructors are more than just teachers. They are coaches, big brothers, motivators, counselors, therapists, and pseudo-parents for many who come from broken homes, broken relationships, and troubled pasts. At this, Petty Officer Brown excelled. I wanted to emulate her and show my recruits that I cared. It was rewarding to see them succeed and become new sailors. I ended up training over six hundred recruits and earned my master training specialist certification.

I faced several challenges while being a drill instructor, presented by the other staff members. The best sailors from the fleet are screened for the job of recruit division commander, which is what drill instructors are called in the Navy. Unfortunately, some are too competitive and only focused on their own advancement opportunities. The recruit division's performance was directly tied to the performance evaluations of the drill instructor, causing many to circumnavigate the competitive system. In other words, they cheated. They provided their recruits with the answers to tests and made behind-the-scenes deals with inspectors to ensure their division ranked among the highest.

Nevertheless, my divisions graduated on their own merit, and I was proud of them for it. When I complained about the crooked staff members to Petty Officer Brown, she replied, "I hate to be the one to crap in your bowl of Wheaties, but if anyone is going to do it, it may as well be me. It's an unfair world, and you have to stand up for what you believe in, even if it costs you. There are bullies everywhere. Look at me; I didn't play their game, and you can see that I haven't been promoted, but it's not about that. It's about taking care of your recruits and training them the right way."

I told her that I was also frustrated about not being able to make Chief Petty Officer as an illustrator because too many sailors had already been over-promoted. Her advice to me was to check in with my illustrator counterpart in Washington State, who was a leadership class instructor who just got selected for photography officer. Photo officers in the Navy were an even more exclusive group of media specialists than illustrators. At that time, the Navy had fewer than sixty total photo officers. They traditionally selected enlisted photographers' mates to advance, but on the most recent selection board, they actually selected an illustrator. "I'm pretty sure a drill instructor would be selected if he applied," she said. I got the message loud and clear. I was emboldened that my drill instructor from years ago now thought that I was ready to become an officer. I applied for the Navy's limited-duty officer program, Photography Officer Designation. "I know you will be selected if you just apply," she said. For the second time in my career, Petty Officer Brown was mentoring me like an angel looking out for me. I got pneumonia again, just like in old times.

I started to think about the bigger picture more often. I studied the scheduling of the training facilities on base and analyzed the number of recruits housed in each barracks. I was fortunate to be a drill instructor in the newest state of the art barracks building on base. At more than sixty million dollars, the Goliath building housed up to thirty-six divisions of recruits, up to eighty-eight recruits each. Within the structure were dining facilities and classrooms so that the recruits no longer had to march to get to where they were going; they could easily spend days indoors and attend class simply by walking down the hall from their barracks room. Automated electronic classrooms provided computers and headphones to each recruit and allowed them to accomplish much of their training through online classes. After studying the way recruit barracks were being filled with incoming recruits and emptied by graduating divisions, I noticed a pattern.

I authored a point paper for the commanding officer demonstrating a more efficient way of loading the barracks and aligning the training facilities on base, titled "*Training Group Consolidation Plan.*" My idea was a huge success, and it changed the way everything was done on the base. There were significant cost savings, and cheating by staff members was disrupted. I was not popular because change is difficult for people, but I was awarded two Navy and Marine Corps Commendation Medals and a Distinguished Leadership Award. I submitted my application for the officer program, and it was time to reenlist and contact my assignment officer for new orders.

My biggest desire after working such long hours for four years was to have a job that afforded me more time with my family. I longed for weekends and holidays off and the opportunity to celebrate birthdays and anniversaries. There is such a thing as devoting too much of yourself to work and neglecting your family, and I was in danger of doing just that. My assignment officer offered me two choices. I could go be stationed on a ship based out of Italy, or I could take shore duty in Hawaii. The answer was obvious. My wife was thrilled about going to Hawaii, and her parents, who were living in Oklahoma, decided to move there too so that they could be there with us and spend time with their granddaughter. Little did I know that this next duty station would present the biggest challenge and transition I had yet experienced in my twelve-year Navy career so far.

CHAPTER 8

BECOMING A NAVY CHIEF AND OFFICER

Do nothing out of selfish ambition
or vain conceit. Rather, in humility
value others above yourselves.
—Philippians 2:3

HAWAII WAS LUSH AND BEAUTIFUL. Double rainbows were a common appearance. I was assigned to an aviation squadron, and we were housed at the Marine Corps Base in Kaneohe on the windward side of the island of Oahu. Streams of water trickled down the mountains like shining diamonds. Green foliage covered the monumental hillsides, and the peninsula cradled exclusive beaches for military families. My wife and I celebrated our fifth wedding anniversary by taking a dinner cruise out of Pearl Harbor, and then we drove to Turtle Bay Resort at the north tip of the island to stay the night. My wife's parents bought a sailboat and lived on it in the harbor. They watched our daughter while we celebrated what seemed like a reward for the long deployments and hard work of being a drill instructor. We flew to the big island and walked on the slopes of the mighty active volcano Kilauea. The beauty of our surroundings was mesmerizing and camouflaged the challenges I was about to face.

It was the summer of 2006, and the Navy finally decided to do away with the job designation of illustrator by merging the job with others. There were four media-related job specialties, consisting of journalist, photographer's mate, illustrator and lithographer. The Navy combined all four jobs into one new specialty called Mass Communication Specialist as part of the restructuring of the larger Navy Public Affairs community of approximately two thousand jobs. It made little difference to me. By now, I had accepted that I would no longer be able to find a posting where I would do illustration work because I was becoming too senior. I did my artwork at home on my own craft table. I had grown as a sailor in many dynamic ways by taking on nontraditional leadership roles. I matured in ways I had not expected and grew to think more about taking care of my subordinates than myself.

I had finished a few small artistic projects for the aircraft squadron when the results for Chief Petty Officer were announced. I had been selected as one of the eleven new Mass Communication Specialist Chief Petty Officers! My commanding officer and command master chief delivered the news. I thought I was in trouble when I was summoned to their offices. Command Master Chief Kendley would become the next positive role model in my professional and personal development as I ascended to the coveted position of Navy chief.

It was a Friday when I carried good news about my promotion home to my wife, and we took the weekend to prepare for the summer chief's initiation. Approximately three hundred Chief Petty Officers stationed throughout the island would participate in training the new Chief Selectees in physical fitness, military drill, and leadership training exclusively designed by and for Navy chiefs. Unfortunately, there are bullies everywhere in life, and they manifested among the ranks of so-called mentors and "genuine chiefs."

The chief's initiation is supposed to be a celebrated training opportunity, but many misguided sailors saw it as an opportunity to get away with hazing. I witnessed the abuse of a female chief selectee, and I reported it. My background as a drill instructor made me keenly aware of the dangers of empowering the wrong sorts of people with too much power over others. I was singled out and teased in front of the other selectees because I had applied for a commissioning program.

A senior chief rescue swimmer thought it was unacceptable that I would become a chief petty officer wanting to convert to officer. He simply didn't understand my intentions. He kept me waiting in the push up position longer than the other selectees, asking me how much money does an officer makes compared with that of an enlisted person, as if I were applying for an officer simply because of the pay raise. I endured extra attention from the Chiefs and was given the nicknames "Ensign" and "En-swine Addison." They called me "Sir" mockingly. I shouted back that I was a chief and that I had earned that title!

I was working late at night at the hangar as a new Chief Petty Officer when the officer selection board results were transmitted. I was one of three sailors selected for Photographic Officer, with a commissioning date of January 2008. I would attend officer indoctrination school, public affairs officer training, and report to the USS Dwight D. Eisenhower as the media department division officer and assistant public affairs officer.

The senior chief rescue swimmer approached me to congratulate me, and he apologized for being rough on me during the initiation. Then he had the nerve to ask me for a copy of my officer application so he could model his application after mine. He too wanted to apply to become an officer, and I simply smiled politely and wished him luck. I hoped he wouldn't get selected. He was the wrong type to be entrusted with leading sailors, in my opinion.

I would spend the next year and a half as a Chief Petty Officer at the squadron, taking ownership of various command programs such as the urinalysis coordinator and unit traffic court magistrate. I participated as a mentor in the next summer's Chief Petty Officer initiation and did it the right way, as a big brother, not as a bully. Throughout the year, Master Chief Kendley continued to mentor me as a new chief and officer selectee. She was like the other guardian angels I was blessed with in my life and provided me with valuable advice. When she saw me working late into the evenings, she reminded me that my family was the only ones who would be there with me when I eventually retired. She was an excellent leader and mentor. She set a positive example for all to emulate.

Another positive role model and guardian angel at that time was Lieutenant Commander Stefan. He was prior enlisted like me, and he was a department head in the squadron. He had powerful connections in the officer community on the island. When he heard about the bullying I was experiencing during Chief's initiation, he networked to arrange a special officer screening board for me with an actual photography officer that he knew to preside on the panel of three commissioned officers. I knew that his endorsement would carry a lot of weight with the selection board when it convened. When the bully chiefs heard about my screening board, they tried to sabotage it by making me do a physical fitness test that same morning. I was late showing up for my board because of the interference, but the officers knew what I was going through, and they saw that I was persistent nonetheless.

When I was at Lieutenant Commander Stefan's desk, I complimented him on a colorful small photo of a little girl wearing an orange pumpkin costume seated between two actual pumpkins. It was an eye-catching image. He said that was the last photo ever taken of his daughter. She died shortly after from a heart ailment. I wanted to show my appreciation for him standing up for me, so late one night I snuck into the hangar and carefully removed that photo from its frame, scanned the image, and emailed it to myself. I returned the photo to its holder as if nothing had happened and rushed home to begin working on a large portrait of the little girl. I made it one of my very best works of art. I placed extra emphasis on her eyes to make her look alive with the light reflecting from her pupils. I used a pastel color palette to show the soft texture of her pumpkin attire. It took me approximately two months to complete it during my off-duty hours at home.

When it was finished, I placed the painting on his chair at his desk at work in the hangar. He wept when he saw it. He approached me with great gratitude, and I told him it was the least I could do for him. He then humbly asked me if I could make another portrait for his other living daughter so that he could have a set of portraits to present to his wife for their anniversary. I was more than happy to accommodate him. I made the second portrait of his other daughter in the same soft manner, with extra emphasis placed on her eyes to bring the image to life. When I presented him with the finished second painting, he was speechless at first. Then he said I wouldn't have to worry about making any plans for my commissioning ceremony because he insisted on being the master of ceremonies for me.

I felt like everything was happening for a reason. I came to believe that artwork should mean much more than mere commercial art and graphic design jobs for an employer. I came to realize that having this talent was a gift, and in turn, it should be used to create meaningful gifts for others. Looking back, the most meaningful works of art I did were individual gifts for people. More importantly, the actions of being a good leader and taking care of people were what really mattered in life. The key lesson I was about to learn is that our actions in life are the brushstrokes of a larger masterpiece.

CHAPTER 9

RETURN TO
THE SEA

The LORD himself will go before you. He
will be with you; He will not leave you or
forget you. Don't be afraid and don't worry.
—Deuteronomy 31:8

MY COMMISSIONING CEREMONY WAS RICH with ceremony and naval tradition in the squadron hangar bay. Flowers were presented to my wife. Lieutenant Commander Stefan presided as the master of ceremonies, just as he had promised. His wife sat next to mine. She gave me a meaningful thank-you card for doing paintings of her daughters. The Navy Band played parade anthems. In the audience were my wife's parents, our daughter, my shipmates from the First Class Petty Officer Association, the Chief Petty Officer's Mess, and my new fellow officers of the officer wardroom.

My commanding officer delivered opening remarks, and I followed with a lengthy speech recalling my thirteen years of service and the lessons I had learned. I thanked my family for their loving support. My wife and commanding officer attached my gold and black officer epaulettes to the shoulders of my summer white uniform, and my officer hat with the gold chin strap and officer's crest replaced my chief's hat. I turned around and received my first salute from a sharp second class petty officer, who was one of my recruits just a few years ago. Life's circles like this one are not coincidences, in my opinion. They are indications of God's bigger picture.

After the ceremony, after thirteen years of being enlisted, I was an officer. Apart from the pay raise, it was a big socioeconomic change for my family. Everything is segregated by the class system in the military. Officers are housed separately on base and aboard the ship. Dining facilities are also separate. There are different rules for liberty. Rank certainly has its privileges in the military. At times, I found it to be a difficult transition to make. I used to be the sailor cleaning officer toilets and carrying their personnel effects onboard ship for them. Now I was on the other side, and whenever I could manage to do so, I showed the enlisted sailors that I remembered where I came from. Each morning at sea, during cleaning stations, the entire crew deep cleans the ship for an hour. Officers supervise the cleaning and make sure the difficult nooks and corners are tended to with polish and elbow grease, but I always helped to show that I was not too good to do my share of the dirty work. This was frowned upon by other officers because it threatened the balance of the class system.

Mustang is a term used to describe officers who start out as enlisted sailors. Like the wild horse, a mustang officer comes from a tougher breeding environment than their thoroughbred counterparts and can be relied upon in difficult situations. Like the free horse, a mustang officer can sometimes revert back to their wild habits. Mustang officers are sometimes found to be guilty of fraternization and other crimes punishable under the uniform code of military justice. I would soon discover that bullies unfortunately exist even in the officer ranks as I embarked on my first tour of duty as a new ensign.

In 2008, I reported to an officer indoctrination school in Newport, Rhode Island. Next, I reported to Fort Meade, Maryland, to attend public affairs officer training. The Navy was making changes to its officer job designators, much like recent changes to the enlisted Mass Communication Specialist merger. Photography officers were being disbanded and merged into the ranks of public affairs officers. My job aboard the aircraft carrier would put me in charge of twenty-five sailors in the media department, and I would be the deputy department head to the ship's public affairs officer. The carrier's media department was responsible for running the ship's television station, daily newspaper, and photography studio. Media sailors created graphics and operated the print shop. They also served as tour guides for visitors. I was proud to think that I used to swab the decks and clean the commodes of this great warship, and now I was back as the ship's photo officer.

In addition to my division officer duties, I would be expected to stand watch aboard the ship in one of the three main watch station areas. There were combat systems, engineering, and bridge team watch stations. I was assigned to the exclusive aircraft carrier bridge team and would soon find myself navigating the ship! We soon left for back-to-back deployments in 2009 and 2010. Learning to stand a bridge watch was like taking a drink of water from a fire hose. There are volumes of navigation rules and nautical theory to digest. Specific captain's standing orders must be memorized. Our captain had twenty-three rules for various situations that he ordered his bridge officers to comply with.

Before any ship navigational event, such as getting underway, anchoring, returning to port, transiting the Suez Canal, and underway replenishments, a navigation safety brief would be held, and each watch officer must demonstrate their proficiency before being allowed to assume their duty and perform the action. Emergency procedures and contingency plans are discussed, along with weather conditions and personnel changes. Safety is the number-one goal of any operation. Collisions at sea, injury, or death can occur when things go wrong.

The sea is unforgiving. The responsibility to study hard, learn the material, and perform the duty of standing a four-hour watch on the bridge of an aircraft carrier weighed heavily on our shoulders. For me, never having had a background in bridge operations, this was a steep learning curve. Compartmentalization was the key to success.

The ability to give the large responsibilities their appropriate amount of attention without letting them pile on top of one another reduced stress levels. I spent what time I could with my division and trusted my noncommissioned officers in my absence when I was up on the bridge. Every night I prayed for the courage and guidance to do the right thing, the right way, for the right reasons.

The bridge windows provided a clear view of the flight deck and the forward half of the large ship. Lookouts reported surface and air contact. The scent of strong coffee permeated the space. Computer monitors and video screens displayed information about the status of the ship. The officer of the deck stood by the captain's chair and was in charge of supervising the bridge team, unless the captain was on the bridge. He usually took his meals on the bridge. The captain's personal cook would impressively carry up the captain's meal several flights of steps, and deliver trays of gourmet finger snacks to the bridge team. The captain, executive officer, and navigator occasionally tested the knowledge of watch standers. My posts were a junior officer of the watch and helm safety officer. One of my responsibilities was to maintain bridge to bridge communications.

During our transit through the Strait of Hormuz, small Iranian boats attempted to swarm the carrier to harass our sailing through international waters. My job was to contact the ships by radio and warn them to stay away. "This is US Warship sixty-nine transiting international waters. Maintain a safe distance from our vessel," I stated firmly. The executive officer called me "the voice of the ship" not only because of my duties on the bridge but also because of my speech writing for the officers when they addressed the crew.

The photo lab was two decks below the hangar bay. When the lookouts saw something suspicious, we called for my photographers to rush to the edge of the ship to take still photos and video of the object for the intelligence department to analyze. I was always energized to join my sailors back down in the media spaces and share my stories from Bridge Watch with them. I was blessed to get to lead such a talented team. I am still proud of them to this day, as many have moved on from the Navy to other successful careers.

During the 2009 combat cruise, we visited France, Bahrain, Jebel Ali, and Portugal. We visited the United Arab Emirates, Turkey, and Italy during the 2010 deployment. I was particularly struck by the ancient city ruins at Pergamum and the well-preserved Aspendos Theater in Turkey. I walked the historic grounds with my camera and took several photos to capture the scene for future paintings. In Italy, I walked to the peak of Mount Vesuvius and explored the excavations of the tragic city of Pompeii, which perished in AD 79. Port visits were welcome breaks from the busy routine of life at sea. These brief visits recharged me and shaped my perspective as a small traveler in a large world.

Officers competed with each other for the best performance and fitness evaluations. The bridge officers were especially competitive because of their close contact and scrutiny by the commanding officer when he was on the bridge. When the captain is away, the cat will play, unfortunately. Some of the officers waited for his absence to fraternize inappropriately with junior enlisted sailors. The captain gave leadership training briefs to the officers in the wardroom once a week. He spoke of the necessity for policies like forceful backup and procedural compliance. One day, his lecture was about the importance of an officer having creativity. This resonated with me deeply as an artist and as a new officer.

One day, the officer of the deck and the conning officer jeopardized the safety of the ship by arguing with each other about how they interpreted the captain's standing orders. I reported the incident to the ship's navigator and found myself ostracized by the other officers for telling on them. I attempted to quit the bridge team because my path upward seemed blocked by the bullies, but another officer I had trained to be a junior officer of the watch found me down in my office. He shut the door and saw that I was crying at my desk. We prayed together, and he said that he admired the courage it took to stand up for what was right. He motivated me to resume my position on the bridge team.

Shortly afterward, we were at battle stations, and I took my place on the bridge. When a less experienced officer relieved me, the captain asked me to stay on the bridge and continue my watch with him. I took it as a compliment to have the captain's confidence. Some things are more meaningful than medals. I was promoted to Lieutenant Junior Grade and progressed to conning the ship. The conning officer is the one who gives speed and direction orders to the helmsman and Lee helmsman of the watch. Conning during flight operations was particularly nerve-racking for me, but at the same time, it was very thrilling to be entrusted with such a great responsibility.

At the end of the 2010 deployment, we pulled into Mayport, Florida, to let family and friends join us on the ship for the final three days of our journey to Norfolk Naval Station. My brother and nephew took advantage of the opportunity. They bunked with us, ate with us, and stood watch alongside us. My brother got to watch me conn the ship during replenishment at sea, where we pulled close alongside the supply ship and connected to it for the transfer of materials. Family members were given tours of the ship, and the sailors were proud to highlight the work they did during deployment. On the flight deck, an air power demonstration showed the family members the capabilities of the ship's mighty air wing.

After homecoming, I went on a secret mission to surprise my mother at her place of work at Aberdeen Proving Ground. Her coworkers contacted me to arrange the ambush. She was having her retirement ceremony, and I would be the secret guest speaker in my Navy officer uniform. Tears of joy ran down her face when I entered the crowded conference room at the Army base. All her coworkers clapped as we embraced. My speech was about thanking her for equipping me, preparing me, and counseling me about life. I remembered her sacrifices as a single parent and the work she did to send me to art school. Public speaking came more naturally to me as a public affairs officer. My trip home was too brief to see my best friend, Joe. We loved sharing stories, but he said he understood and we would get together the next time I was in town.

I managed to fit college classes into my heavy work schedule to work on my bachelor's degree. Usually, a four-year college degree is required to be an officer, but I was commissioned through a unique Navy Limited Duty Officer program. Limited duty officer meant that I was commissioned based on technical merit in the media field, and a college degree was desired but not necessarily required. Since I was a limited-duty officer, I was limited to postings specifically coded for photography officers.

Life on a ship at sea is like being in a great house of learning. There is so much to learn about ship systems, warfare operations, and navigation. There is also the opportunity to take college classes on the ship. When the photography officers were disbanded and merged into public affairs officers, the four-year degree suddenly became a requirement, and we were given a grace period to complete it. Some officers never finished their degrees, but it was a matter of honor for me. Furthering my education was one of my core goals for joining the Navy.

During deployment, I completed English classes and my favorite class of all time, world literature. Mr. Maik was one of the civilian teachers contracted to sail with the ship's crew. He was an expert traveler and familiar with the ancient archaeological locations around the Mediterranean Sea. We studied Homer's Iliad and Odyssey. We learned about the Vatican and Roman Colosseum just prior to visiting Naples, and then we took tours by bus to Rome to see the sites we discussed in class in person. I was awestruck at the massive cross erected at the Colosseum as a tribute to Christians who perished there long ago.

The Vatican was impressively adorned with statues and beautiful artwork. The opportunity to see the Sistine Chapel was a once-in-a-lifetime experience. I was inspired by seeing the work of the masters in person to not only resume my humble artwork but to dedicate the purpose of my artwork and my acts in life to glorifying God. I felt that artwork should be a meaningful gift and not be commercially sold as it is in advertising. I began to see a bigger picture for my sense of purpose. I felt motivated to spread the good message about God through my deeds and words so that others may find the hope and peace that I have been blessed with. I felt extremely humbled and realized that my education in life was just beginning. Maybe there was much more to life than drawing and painting pictures.

CHAPTER 10

AFGHANISTAN

For he will command his angels concerning
you to guard you in all your ways.
—Psalm 91:11

IN 2011, MY CONVERSION TO public affairs officer from photography officer was official. Options for orders were far more limited for officers because there were fewer jobs to fill than enlisted
positions. I was blessed to receive shore duty orders to Millington,
Tennessee, at the US Navy Recruiting Command's Headquarters as
the branch manager for the creative services branch of the marketing
and advertising department. Here, I would lead the finest illustrators
in the Navy. They were a team of civilians and military experts in
graphic design, as well as photographers and videographers, who produced commercials and recruiting advertisements designed to attract
people to join the Navy. I may not have been doing the illustration
work hands-on myself, but I could not envision a better place to
work at this point in my career.

That summer, I received the terrible news from my half sister
that my best friend, Joseph W. Thomas, had passed away. He died

alone at York Hospital in Pennsylvania from complications related to his lifelong battle with diabetes. I recalled that the last time we spoke, we thought we always had another time to catch up with each other. We were wrong. I regretted not telling him all the things he meant to me. He was there to remind me to see the bigger picture as a new dad when I was a teenage parent. We dreamed of starting a band and becoming rock stars. I was angry at my decision to stay in the Navy and miss so much of life at home. I cried wet, flowing tears for hours. My daughter gave me a teddy bear and said she named it Joe for me. I traveled home on leave to simply stand at his grave, where he was laid to rest next to his parents. My coworkers sent flowers.

My three-year dream posting of a shore duty assignment was interrupted eight months into my job with a new set of orders to go serve with an even more exclusive team. I was handpicked to join a provincial reconstruction team that would serve in the remote and arduous location of Farah Province in Afghanistan, in the desert terrain along the Iranian border. The team was led by a Navy SEAL commander and senior chief petty officer, along with an Army civil affairs lieutenant colonel. Other Navy officers selected for this unique assignment included an aviator, a medical officer, and Navy construction battalion engineer officers.

My role was to be the public affairs officer for the team and a liaison officer for Afghan counterparts in the telecommunications and postal fields, as well as the advisor for the Afghan Farah Province minister of Information and Culture. Army infantry soldiers would provide security for us while we went on missions to extend the reach of the Afghan government to remote regions of the war-torn country's population. We were in a fight against the Taliban for the confidence of the Afghan people. The provincial reconstruction teams oversaw construction projects such as medical clinics and wells for villages in need. They worked with local authorities to repair roads from the blasts of improvised explosive devices. Our commander met regularly with the governor of the province to discuss security matters.

The mission began with training in Indiana, where the twelve provincial reconstruction teams were formed and trained for three months before rotating into the theater of operations to relieve the current teams on the ground. The training was intense and comprehensive because we would be operating remotely, beyond the immediate reach of many of the NATO assets in Afghanistan. Each team member qualified for the use of small arms, and the larger crew served weapons. The weapons training more than made up for the lack of training I received during my deployment to the former Yugoslavia. Cold winter days and nights were spent on Army firing ranges designed to simulate potential combat scenarios we could face. We slept together in open bay barracks and in tents, and I missed the team of fine illustrators I was meant to lead at Navy recruiting headquarters. We practiced convoy operations and casualty evacuations. We conducted a nine-mile rucksack march loaded down with the weight of body armor, battle gear, and weapons. My feet were never so sore, and I gained a whole new sense of appreciation for my Army counterparts.

This would be a far different deployment experience for the Navy officers on the team. There were no shipboard facilities. The intense weeklong combat lifesaver first aid course reminded us of the danger we faced. We were joined midway through training by representatives from the US State Department, the US Department of Agriculture, and the US Assistance for International Development. Just weeks before completing our final training project, I was struck down with pneumonia again. I was hospitalized at a local medical facility, and my wife and daughter drove from Tennessee to be at my bedside. My pneumonia was so severe that I was sent home to finish recovering for the next several weeks while my unit deployed without me.

My hospitalization gave me time to think about my purpose for this mission. I tried to see a bigger picture. I started out wanting merely to do illustration work as an artist for the Navy, and here I was sick again. Did I make the right decision by staying in the military? I prayed for a sense of purpose. I started to feel better after a few weeks. I visited my colleagues at the creative services office. It was business as usual, and everyone was working on routine advertising art. There was no crisis. My training prepared me for the worst possible situations. I felt a deep sense of responsibility to join my brothers and sisters in the Provincial Reconstruction Team. By now, they were already engaged in working with Afghan counterparts who sorely needed help in places where the Taliban held influence. I knew I belonged overseas with them.

My doctor cleared me to deploy, and I returned to Camp Atterbury in Indiana to retrieve my gear and my weapons, which had been placed in storage. I was driven to the airport to begin my long journey halfway around the world to catch up with my unit. I flew to Baltimore Washington International Airport to what is known as the "Deployment Gateway" at the international terminal there. From there, I flew to Germany, Qatar, and then to Kyrgyzstan, and finally Afghanistan. My shipmates in my unit were happy to see me. I checked in with my commander for an update and got to work.

Farah Province in Afghanistan looks like the surface of another planet. Jagged rock formations resemble craters, and forbidding mountainous peaks are laced throughout the desert terrain. The temperatures in the summer months are among the hottest in the world. We recorded a temperature of one hundred twenty-seven degrees Fahrenheit. The small outpost where we lived and worked was called a forward operating base. The location was in disrepair, and we spent time and effort fixing it up. Everyone chipped in to build decks, porch covers, and picnic tables. The civil affairs lieutenant colonel had a green thumb and cultivated flowers next to the assembly room designated for meeting with Afghans, called a Shura room.

My coworker and singular subordinate were like another guardian angel in my life. Staff Sergeant Lovelady was a seasoned US Air Force Combat Camera photojournalist. He regularly went on expeditionary assignments, often accompanying special warfare operators. He trained me to take my own photographs and showed me what he was capable of from the start. He needed me as a public affairs officer as much as I needed him. We made the best team I experienced in my military career. Together, we released thousands of images and multimedia products for a worldwide audience, making our unit one of the most well-known in the theater of operations. An Italian general in our chain of command commended our public affairs activities.

The deployment was the most difficult I had experienced for many reasons. On my birthday, I read a long letter from my mother. She felt the need to confess to me that she almost had an abortion with me because her doctor recommended it. Her doctor feared that there would be birth defects because of the radiation from X-rays she received before she knew she was pregnant. She reluctantly decided to keep the baby, and her birthday message to me was that I should feel lucky to be alive. I was distracted by her letter, to say the least. It reinforced my belief in pro-life decisions and policies. I did indeed feel grateful to be alive, and I thanked God for it. I contemplated all the places and people I interacted with.

The next several months became a blur of daily missions. Sometimes we complete two missions in a day. We traveled in heavily armored vehicles called MRAPs (Mine Resistant Ambush Protected) due to the threat from improvised explosive devices. We were not always welcome. Children threw rocks at us and sometimes scored a direct hit on the gunner up in the turret of the vehicle. Once, while traveling through a village with very high mud brick walls, a dead snake was tossed into the turret with the gunner. The motto of forces in Afghanistan was "exercise restraint and when directed, win decisively." The restraint and professionalism of the very young infantry soldiers deserve special mention. Their presence definitely saved lives and kept violence from escalating when we traveled to meet our Afghan counterparts. I felt safe among them and was successful because of their protection.

2012 was an especially dangerous year in Afghanistan because of the rampant increase in suicide attacks against coalition forces. Our security posts were catching infiltrators crawling low in attempts to breach the perimeter of our small forward operating base. A tragedy struck when two United States servicemen stationed at our base paid the ultimate price for service to their country. A United States Marine Corps Staff Sergeant and a US Navy Hospital Corpsman First Class were shot and killed by a local Afghan assassin posing as an Afghan trainee. Both brave servicemen were only thirty-six years old, and both were fathers just a few weeks from going home at the end of deployment. We rendered honors called a "ramp ceremony" for the fallen under the cover of darkness as the plane came to carry them home. This was the lowest point of deployment, and it hit many of us particularly hard. Especially touched by this terrible loss was Hospital Corpsman Petty Officer Second Class medic, who witnessed the carnage from attacks during deployment up close, and it left a tremendous scar on him. Our hearts and prayers went out to their families. Sometimes the cost of service to the country is everything.

I returned home hypervigilant. I felt like I needed to hurry back to Afghanistan for the adrenaline rush from the danger and also to gain a sense of completion. The urge to go back is self-destructive. I found myself exhibiting fearful behavior, always afraid of an imminent attack. I showed up to work extra early to check office spaces before I felt safe to be there. I slept odd hours on the couch in the living room. My anxiety was high, and my temper was short. I felt the uncontrollable urge to walk the perimeter of our house to make sure it was safe at night. I contacted the military hotline to speak with a counselor because I knew something wasn't right. This deployment experience profoundly affected me. A behavioral health therapist at the medical clinic counseled me weekly and prescribed medication to help with anxiety. I gradually returned to a version of my former self that was especially thankful to be alive. I left part of myself in Afghanistan. I wanted to go back and do more work that felt unfinished.

I had a year remaining on my orders in Tennessee. I spent 2013 completing my bachelor of science degree, majoring in communication and administration management. I volunteered to assist the headquarters chief of staff as chairman of the Navy Ball Committee. Each year, on the anniversary of the Navy's birthday, the service celebrates with a traditional dinner and dance party featuring the United States Navy Band. The committee is responsible for fundraising to offset the cost of tickets for service members and for venue selection and party details. I empowered my team to be creative, and the result was the best ball in recent memory at that time. We paid special tribute to those who sacrificed to serve in the sea service, including those who deployed on the ground to places like Iraq and Afghanistan in the war on terror.

CHAPTER 11

SHORE DUTY

Heal me, O LORD, and I shall be healed; save
me, and I shall be saved: for Thou art my praise.
—Jeremiah 17:14

IN 2014, I RECEIVED NEW orders from the Navy Region Southwest Headquarters in San Diego, California. Shortly after reporting, I got pneumonia again. I was a special projects officer for various public affairs concerns, such as the Navy liaison to the San Diego Chargers football team and the San Diego Padres baseball team. The major sports teams wanted to show their support to the military by offering tickets for sailors in the area and including the service members in the opening ceremonies at some of the games. I had a new sense of appreciation for the relaxed pace of shore duty work following the busy tempo of deployments. I valued the opportunity to be with my family in the evenings and on weekends. It was a blessing of healing and recovery to be stationed in beautiful southern California.

My wife and I made the decision to begin homeschooling our daughter rather than move her from school to school every couple of years. Life as a military dependent is tough. It made our daughter resilient, but she missed out on having steady friendships like most children her age. She was also diagnosed with special medical needs so we were enrolled in the Navy's exceptional family member program to ensure appropriate medical facilities were available at our duty station assignments. We kept in touch with my son as best as we could. He moved around a lot and went through a period of finding his own way as a young adult. Military service takes a huge toll on family members. They deserve my eternal gratitude for supporting me through twenty-six years of active-duty service.

San Diego offered splendid opportunities for recreation with the family. The natural beauty of the beaches and Pacific Ocean and attractions like SeaWorld made for wonderful memories. We enjoyed several months of a relatively easy workload and ample free time to explore the Medieval Times restaurant in Los Angeles, participate in the San Diego Comic Convention, and a Star Trek convention in Las Vegas, Nevada. The local military bases offered bowling, swimming, and movie theaters for military families. It was a precious time to recharge for the challenges ahead.

New challenges came swiftly, though. Shakespeare wrote in Hamlet, "When sorrows come, they come not as single spies, but in battalions." I suffered a transient ischemic attack, which is also known as a ministroke. Imaging of my brain revealed several white matter lesions. I thanked God that my symptoms of blurry vision, a droopy left side of my face, and neck and shoulder pain only lasted a few days. A nurse case manager was assigned, and I made a commitment to improve my health. I was fully recovered several weeks later, just in time to answer duty's call again.

One by one, the military installations within our six state areas of responsibility began to lose their public affairs officers for various reasons, leaving critical, unexpected personnel gaps. I was dispatched to be the public affairs officer for Naval Submarine Base Point Loma for several weeks. Next, I was sent to be the public affairs officer for Naval Air Station Lemoore in Northern California for several months until a civilian was hired to fill the vacancy. After that, I was assigned to be the public affairs officer for Naval Base San Diego, which is the largest Navy base on the West Coast and home to one hundred fifty units with more than fifty ships on thirteen piers.

I grew professionally and fine-tuned my skills as a versatile and independent public affairs officer. My extra duty in San Diego kept me much busier than I expected. I worked long hours and weekends and spent a lot of time away from home while working at other bases. That's when my assignment officer contacted me with a new set of special orders.

In 2015, a Chairman of the Joint Chief of Staff needed a special job filled. It would be to undergo advanced training, including language school, learn to speak Dari, and deploy to Afghanistan as a military advisor and cultural expert in the Afghanistan Pakistan Hands Program (AFPAK Hands). The assignment officer said she believed I would be a good fit because of my previous deployment experience. I felt a calling deep inside me again. It felt much like a hand guiding me at a crossroads. I volunteered to fill the position and told my wife and coworkers. I accepted the orders and reported for duty in Washington, DC, at the Washington Navy Yard. I was fitted for concealed body armor and given a long list of schools to attend to receive the best training possible to be successful in Kabul, Afghanistan's capital city.

Language training lasted through most of 2016. By the time I graduated, I was proficient at reading, writing, and speaking Dari. I never imagined I would be able to learn another language, but the intensive one-on-one training accelerated the speed of learning. My language instructors were once doctors and executives in the Afghan government before fleeing the Taliban to seek sanctuary in the United States. They taught me not only their language but also about their culture, religion, holidays, and traditions. I learned the importance of taking time to sip a cup of hot green tea to build rapport while asking about the welfare of each other's family. I was a step closer to becoming ready to deploy as an AFPAK Hand.

I attended additional schools and received the latest anti-terrorism training and high-risk-of-capture preparation available. A major milestone in the training pipeline was to earn a Master of Arts in Strategic Security Studies with a focus on South and Central Asia from the National Defense University's College of International Security Affairs. My thesis was about how the American volunteer force model of recruiting was a poor fit for the Afghan culture in the midst of a war. I defended my thesis and graduated in June 2017. The school year was filled with classes about military history and global strategy. We attended leadership lectures from guest speakers such as Colin Powell, Condoleezza Rice, and Newt Gingrich. Field trips to the United Nations in New York City and Gettysburg National Military Park sharpened our strategic perspectives. I was finally ready to deploy to Kabul, Afghanistan, as a military advisor.

The long journey began with heartfelt goodbyes to my family. We knew this deployment was coming during the intense training process, and in a way, it was a relief to finally have the painful moment of separation come so that we could begin counting down the three hundred sixty-five days until homecoming. My son wrote a meaningful farewell note and tucked it away in the pocket of one of my bags of gear. He said that he was proud of me and hoped we could spend more time together when I returned. My weapons case and seven bags of equipment weighed down the airport luggage dolly at Baltimore International Airport. I mailed ahead additional items I would need that I learned about from my previous deployment to Afghanistan. You have to assume that there are no supplies available there and take everything you need for such a trip. My assignment in theater was finalized, and I learned that I would be working with NATO Psychological Operations (PSYOPS). Captain Green was the officer in charge of the AFPAK Hands program. He met me at the terminal to say good luck and that he would be in touch if I needed him. I hold his leadership in high regard to this day. He genuinely cared about the officers he led.

Touchdown at Bagram Air Base in Afghanistan was an eye-opener. The security situation had deteriorated dramatically since I was there with the troop surge five years ago. New arrivals were required to watch a video demonstrating the proper duck-and-cover procedures for frequent incoming rocket attacks. The dwindled footprint of American forces was evident in the empty barracks structures that were once occupied by numerous coalition forces. The final leg of my trip was by helicopter, approximately thirty minutes south of Hamid Karzai International Airport on the edge of Kabul, where I reported to my assignment at the PSYOPS compound. The air was dry, and the surrounding mountains were clearly jagged. At 5,873 feet elevation, Kabul is one of the highest capital cities. I was tired from carrying my weapons and multiple bags of equipment from the terminal to my barracks room. I straightened up my uniform and reported to the commander.

CHAPTER 12

AFGHANISTAN AGAIN

The Lord keeps you from all harm and watches
over your life. The Lord keeps watch over you
as you come and go, both now and forever.
—Psalm 121:78

MY WORK ROUTINE BEGAN IMMEDIATELY as the new coun-
terpropaganda officer. I worked with the target audience analysis
team that directed communication efforts for the unit. I referenced
my thesis from my master's degree when working on messaging for
recruiting initiatives for the Afghan security forces. I began advis-
ing the Afghan National Police at the Ministry of Interior headquarters located down the street from the airport. I met the local Afghan
employees at the PSYOPS unit who worked as interpreters and focus
group coordinators for our communication products. These brave
Afghans risked their safety and the safety of their families to work
alongside coalition forces. Their noble dreams of peace for their

country and their fight to survive decades of war touched me deeply. My Dari language skills made me an instant celebrity with them.

I spent time each day getting to know our Afghan coworkers. We shared tea and lunch meals, and I told them about my home and family. We had much in common. The goal of safety and security for our families and the desire for a peaceful future for our children are the same. It wasn't long before I was sought out for my endorsement as an American military officer for their applications for Special Immigrant Visas. The highly coveted program selects loyal Afghan applicants to travel and work in the United States but requires a lengthy appraisal by a frontline American military officer supervisor. I was reluctant at first because I was new to the experience. I eventually wrote and endorsed dozens of reports. Today, six Afghan families are living and prospering safely here in America as a result of my efforts. Looking back on the deployment experience as a whole, this was the most meaningful outcome I could ever have hoped for for them.

This final deployment took everything I had. The first blow came on September 27, 2017, when we endured rocket attacks all day long as the United States Secretary of Defense visited Kabul. More than forty rockets were launched and failed to hit the dignitary's plane, but they successfully damaged the surrounding airport. We sheltered in a bunker as an automated announcement system warned of each inbound rocket, stating, "Warning, incoming rocket, seek cover…" over and over again throughout the day as the blasts thundered far and near. Kabul was much more dangerous than it had been during the years of Allied occupation leading up to this point. With fewer coalition troops on the ground, the roads were no longer safe between the airport and the International Security Assistance Force headquarters located in the heart of the city.

Helicopter taxis were the primary means of travel between the two major hubs of activity. I always had a fear of heights, and the Blackhawk helicopters flew with the side doors open for the door gunners. When the helicopters banked and turned, the city below rolled up into view until we landed at our destination. The only driving I did during deployment was limited to on base only as a collateral duty postal officer responsible for handling American mail for the unit. I shared the mini-missions with my coworker and friend, Polish Major Tomasz Tabaczynski. He honored me with a surprise. I was selected to receive a Polish Army Bronze Medal for service as an allied partner in theater to the Polish Forces. I was deeply moved by this honor. Our unit was mostly made up of Romanian soldiers, but there were also Polish, Italian, and American troops. I became dear friends with them all and admired the leadership of our commander, Colonel Petre.

The second punch in the gut during deployment came on Christmas. My father was in the hospital and was not expected to live after suffering an aneurysm. I phoned the hospital to speak with him and told him I was on my way home on emergency leave. His last words to me were, "Please hurry." I checked out with my commander and rushed to the helicopter for my flight to Bagram Airfield. By the time my helicopter landed, he had passed away. My head was distracted with thoughts of regret. I chose to distance myself and my family from him as an adult. He never met his granddaughter. Memories of childhood abuse haunted me and confused my soul. When I arrived at John F. Kennedy Airport in New York, a police officer escorted me off the plane and through the busy airport that was overcrowded with holiday travelers. She screamed, "Out of the way, American serviceman is coming through!" and the crowd respectfully parted so that I could make the next available flight to Baltimore on time.

I grieved with my siblings and made financial arrangements for my father. We gathered at my half brother's house, where he had photo albums of the family with pictures of Dad spread throughout. My mother's health had deteriorated from lung cancer, and she was on oxygen and in a wheelchair. We gathered around her in front of the Christmas tree to take a photo. Being home on emergency leave for two weeks is bittersweet. I was shell-shocked by the rocket attack and hypervigilant. I was amped up on the adrenaline that comes with being ready to respond to an attack, and my anxiety grew out of control. I prayed for calm and safety as I made my way back through the long series of flights to return to my station in Kabul. When I returned to Afghanistan, I was given a new assignment. I was now the sole military advisor for the Ministry of Defense Public Affairs General and his staff because the previous military advisors for public affairs rotated home without replacements.

One of my first tasks as a member of the newly formed Ministerial Advisory Group for Defense Staff was to escort a group of seven Afghan Army Colonels by air for a disaster response training exercise to Kandahar as a military attaché. My cultural training and Dari language skills made me instant friends with the colonels, who were, in my opinion, very brave and professional and even had funny sense of humor. During the weeklong trip, I realized that the Afghan troops needed time off on Friday to pray because it was their holy day. The American planning officers they were working with did not allow for this in their agenda until I intervened. I found a mosque on the base where they could pray, and while walking back from the mosque, the senior Afghan officer said I was now a brother to them and an honorary member of the village of Shewaki, where most of them were from. Then each of the other officers took turns pledging their brotherhood with me, and we all became much closer after that. I was honored to have earned the friendship of these fiercely loyal warriors.

The third devastating blow of deployment came on Saturday on February 24, 2018. The morning rain was drizzling through a cold, damp mist. I was walking "outside the wire" to leave the perimeter of the headquarters on a mission to advise an Afghan general when a suicide bomber detonated his vest just outside the main gate. The blast rocked me, and I was in a state of shock as I returned inside the base. The base alarm system was blaring "shelter in place" instructions in routine fashion. I walked slowly back to my desk in the small public affairs office building. A British colleague asked, "Are you okay mate?" I nodded and stared at the surveillance video footage of the carnage left on the street. I was numb.

My post-traumatic stress symptoms intensified. What I would learn later is that the effects of trauma are cumulative and become more intense. I coped with the stress and anxiety much like I did when I was a child dealing with child abuse. Food stuck in my throat.

I ground my teeth hard when I slept and clenched my jaw shut throughout each day. I took ibuprofen for the pain the clenching caused. I had violent nightmares and slept for only two to three hours at a time due to hypervigilance. The fourth blow during deployment came unexpectedly from my assignment officer, who was contacting me with news that the AFPAK Hands program was being shut down and that it was time to negotiate a new set of orders. He said it was unfortunate that I volunteered for this assignment as it was no longer considered a valued tour of duty for career progression. I felt shocked and betrayed. This was a completely different story from when I was drafted for this arduous, supposedly significant career milestone.

Day after day, I walked the streets of downtown Kabul along with a small guardian angel group of infantry soldiers who were trained to escort the military advisors. Beggars and children hovered outside the main gate of the headquarters, hoping for handouts of candy, food, or money. I told them in Dari to keep it clear that it was too dangerous to be there. I helped coordinate new audiovisual gear to equip a press conference room for the Afghan Ministry of Defense spokesmen and coordinated a communication conference for Afghan public information officers. Each day seemed like an eternity of waiting for the next attack to happen. Attacks throughout the city and in other provinces were rampant, with staggering casualty counts. The future of Afghanistan was uncertain.

I became addicted to analyzing news reports and communication plans. I was frustrated at people who were not interested in foreign affairs. Becoming bilingual opened my mind to thinking outside my comfort zone. Working alongside the brave Afghans reminded me to look at a picture bigger than my own career and my own country. We were striving toward a vision of peace and prosperity for future generations to live with freedom and safety. I was frustrated that I would not be replaced at the end of my deployment because my program was being shut down. There was still so much to do. Saying goodbye to the Afghan generals and colonels in their offices was a sad occasion. They presented me with a certificate of appreciation and an engraved ballpoint pen etched with "Major Ben" on it.

I left part of myself in Afghanistan and brought the conflict home inside me. I was changed again. I told stories about deployment to my family members, who tried to understand, but without being there, it was difficult for them to connect. I found that talking with other veterans was beneficial because they had been there and endured the same hardships while struggling for the same goals. The troop withdrawal and subsequent fall of Afghanistan to the Taliban were heart-wrenching. Did we fail? Did we leave our Afghan brothers to suffer on their own? Several Afghans contacted me, asking me to help them escape. I was only able to help a few families resettle in the United States, but perhaps that was the main thing that mattered, that is, if it was possible to feel good about the deployments to Afghanistan.

CHAPTER 13

POST-TRAUMATIC STRESS DISORDER

And who is he that will harm you, if ye
be followers of that which is good?
—1 Peter 3:13

AT THE END OF THE deployment, expeditionary Navy sailors were transitioned home via a stop for morale and decompression in Germany at the Warrior Transition Program. This was a waypoint designed to decompress for a week and receive briefs and lectures about staying safe when reuniting with family and friends back in the United States. The program highlight for many of the returning warriors was a bus ride to a local German town to be tourists and enjoy the European atmosphere and hospitality of the village shops and restaurants. I declined to participate. I hid in my barracks room. The medical officer on duty evaluated me and said that it was beyond her scope to provide me with the care I needed for post-traumatic stress disorder, but I would surely receive help for it when I returned home.

I returned home in August 2018. Eager to start thirty days of hard-earned leave and be with my family, I hid at home. I was antisocial. I didn't want to venture away from the house, even to go shopping for groceries. Loud noises startled me easily. I hid in my bedroom, just as I did when I was a child. My family walked on eggshells around me. Anxiety made my heart race high. I needed help. Every road intersection was a potential ambush site. In parking lots, I was an embarrassment for my wife because I was analyzing every car door slam as a potential threat. I returned home from outings exhausted from anxiety attacks and feeling the need to protect my family. I reported myself in need of behavioral health assistance to my medical clinic, and a referral was put into the system.

It took six months for the referral to manifest into an actual appointment with a provider at Walter Reed National Military Medical Center's Behavioral Health Department due to a surge in patients and lack of sufficient number of providers to care for them all. My doctor said that she was frustrated at having to carry the caseload of other doctors who left the practice, and she had to decide which patients she would see instead of others.

My newest assignment as a liaison officer at the Pentagon had the primary benefit of being physically close to home. I felt that it was time to retire. I could no longer endure the duties required of service with my distracting anxiety and hypervigilance, knowing that my recent deployment was unvalued by my chain of command. It took time for access to medical care to become available, but when it did manifest, significant damage had already been done to my psyche and to my body.

Grinding my teeth each night as I suffered through nightmares led to wearing them down so much that my dentist suggested affixing crowns to them, but risky crown lengthening surgery would need to be performed on all my teeth. The first surgery was on the three upper back teeth on my right mandible. Gum tissue and bone were cut away to expose more tooth surfaces for crowns to be affixed. We did not take into account the severity of my nightmares and tooth grinding, known as bruxism. The night after the surgery, I had a particularly bad nightmare about suicide bombers and bit down hard on a mouth guard that had twisted its position in my mouth and fractured my facial bone.

I woke up to a swollen face and a bloodshot right eye. I reported to the emergency room and was sent home to take ibuprofen for pain. I did not know it at the time, but a pathway of infection opened up to allow oral bacteria called Actinomyces israelii to invade the rest of my body. I developed a bone infection called osteomyelitis in the tissue of my mouth and began to suffer a wide range of infectious symptoms, such as night sweats and fevers. It took doctors at Walter Reed Hospital seven months to diagnose me with actinomycosis because it is notoriously difficult to culture and catch as the culprit behind the infection. It is also very difficult to treat. My body was flooded with antibiotics for sixteen months. I ended up losing all my upper teeth and was fitted with a denture and mouth guard. A year later, I was diagnosed with primary immunodeficiency disease and prescribed weekly immunoglobulin infusions for specific antibody deficiency. It explained why the actinomycosis spread and why I got pneumonia so many times.

Another blow to my resilience came when my mother passed away in January 2019. The hospice nurse told us that her time was near, and as a family, we gathered around her. Half of me was still in Afghanistan. My mind was torn apart by grief at losing my mother, an unreconciled relationship with my father, who also recently passed away, and the fact that my decision to join the military for a career meant that I would not be home very much. The brief periods of leave that I spent with my wife and children were poor consolation compared to our collective sacrifices for my service to the country. At least I knew my parents loved me and were proud of me for elevating my life by joining the military, but there was bitterness too, at the separation, and I missed special moments over the years. Tell loved ones how you feel before it is too late.

It was during this time that I also began to suffer severe sciatic nerve pain from my lower back down to my left leg. Spinal stenosis crippled my ability to walk without the assistance of a cane. I was referred to the Navy Wounded Warrior Program and accepted into their care. They appointed a care team and a nurse practitioner to monitor my progress, assist me with things like getting a handicapped parking pass, and begin the paperwork to start the process of convening a medical board, which would determine my fitness to continue to serve or not. The board convened a year later, and I was medically retired from active duty and transferred to the Temporary Disability Retired List. Another year passed, and I was transferred to permanent retired status.

A small surprise retirement ceremony was held in my honor by my commander and the Chief Petty Officers Association at my final duty station, Defense Media Activity, at Fort Meade, Maryland. My two deployments to Afghanistan were marked with two Meritorious Service Medals, and my career was punctuated with a Defense Meritorious Service Medal, which was given at the ceremony. My wife and children were present, and we were deeply honored by the sanctity of the service. They each received letters of appreciation for their support of me during my career.

On my birthday in August 2021, I watched on the news as the final American forces withdrew from Hamid Karzai International Airport in Kabul, Afghanistan, with spectacular coverage that depicted Afghans clinging for life to the outside of the last departing aircraft. I wept. I know I am not the only veteran who feels this way. I believe service members will continue to cope with tours of duty there for years to come. It will be in the hands of historians to judge our efforts there as time goes on.

CHAPTER 14

HOMECOMING

Howbeit Jesus suffered him not, but saith
unto him, go home to thy friends, and tell
them how great things the Lord hath done
for thee, and hath had compassion on thee.
—Mark 5:19

TWENTY-SIX YEARS LATER, I WAS finally retired, living at our
house near my hometown, and recovering from my long adventures.
My uniforms are tucked away in storage. I traveled long and far.
Nearly four years of my life were spent on the ocean. I spent five
years living abroad. I have visited countless countries. My hometown
is much smaller, but being home now is far sweeter than it has ever
tasted. The adventure of life continues at home, as I am now able
to fully focus on my children, family, and health. I see the world
through a different lens now because I caught a glimpse of a much
bigger picture. I will forever be humbled by those brave veterans who
made the ultimate sacrifice and those who lost more than I did in
service to our country.

I have a deeper respect for family members who served in the military. Many fellow veterans, teachers, and friends helped me along the way. Perhaps angels in disguise are responsible and deserve my gratitude. It is a great gift for me to be able to reflect on all that I have experienced and to share my story. My quest to become an artist led me down a long road rich with fond memories. Life as a veteran is different than I expected it would be due to my ongoing struggle with post-traumatic stress disorder. I stay fixated on the news about happenings in the Middle East. Nightmares, anxiety disorder, and hypervigilance are challenges, but my faith in God helps to fortify me when I realize that everything is part of a bigger picture. The Veteran's Administration health care providers and my civilian medical doctors have been a great team and continue to work with me. There is a clear need for behavioral health professionals, and I hope that these vital services can continue to meet the demand signal from those in need of help.

My hope is to tell my story about service and sacrifice. I earned a Master of Fine Arts in Creative Writing to gain the confidence to tell my tale. Taking college classes online again gave me a sense of accomplishment that is therapeutic. I want to show that God's plans for me were clearly different and far grander than my own humble ambitions of wanting to be an artist. Art is an important part of my life. I am proud of the work I have completed and gifted away. My painting of the seven bowls of God's wrath being poured out by seven angels was selected to be displayed at the local art association's annual show. I took my son to see it in the gallery on opening day and gave it to him as a gift afterward.

I feel that God was with me from the very beginning and continues to shepherd me. Through prayer, I find my faith growing and my relationship with God closer than ever. I am afforded the rare luxury in life of being able to look back on my adventures and analyze where I came from and where I have yet to go. I feel compelled to share my story for the benefit of others. Perhaps my story will help inspire young readers who find themselves in abusive homes. I understand what it is like to dream of escape. I can attest to the rewards of answering a call to serve. While my remaining years remain uncertain, one thing is crystal clear to me. Our actions in life and our relationships with others are the brushstrokes of God's masterpiece.

I feel that God's gift of art in my life was meant to connect with others. I felt a calling to reach other veterans and use art when I could as a gift to make someone smile. I presented the pastor of my mother's church with a painting of the exterior of the historic church building. I enjoy making people smile with small acts of kindness and giving paintings to my relatives and close friends. I hope to be remembered by the family motto, "To Serve is to Live," because I believe that in serving others, we find purpose and meaning in life. I enjoy keeping in touch with my Afghan counterparts who made it to the United States and following their journey to become new US citizens.

I hope my children and family can understand why I wasn't always there and why I came home a different person. I am eternally grateful to God for the precious experience of life and the blessings of seeing a small part of His plan unfold. I am also thankful for the many guardian angels laced throughout my life who offered help and guidance at just the right times when I needed assistance. I pray that they will continue to be available for me and our children. The bullies we face in life have no power when we consider God's greater glory and stand with each other in righteous endeavors. There was always a positive role model for me to turn to if I could just open my eyes to see it. As shining lights, we will be targets of the enemy, but together with our shared values, we are stronger.

There are stories with far more bravery and adventure than my own humble experience. We should find a way to capture as much information as we can before it is lost to time. I encourage those considering a career in the military to carefully weigh the benefits against the potential costs. Find veterans and talk with them about their experiences. My hope is for future generations to continue to answer the call and serve their country with the same zeal, fidelity, and professionalism that we did, so that the torch of protector is always carried by people with good values and intentions.

I feel that there is hope for children in disadvantaged situations as long as they cling to God and Christian values. I believe that the effects of trauma are cumulative and become more intense with time. My advice is to seek help early and often. Art therapy continues to be a positive outlet for me. The Wounded Warrior Program offers adaptive sports and opportunities to meet and socialize with other veterans.

God elevated my life through a career in the military. I learned to think beyond my desire to become an artist and consider that my interactions with others during my lifetime were brush strokes of a different type. Life's path may not always be clear, but we can find peace knowing that God's masterpiece continues to be painted through our actions.

CHAPTER 15

POEMS

May the God of hope fill you with all joy and
peace in believing, so that by the power of
the Holy Spirit you may abound in hope.
—Romans 15:13

Separate Spaces

A large house divides us,
splits our lives into two.
Mobile phone messaging,
reminders of what to do.
Strangers think us queer,
I miss you all the way.
Estranged yet so near,
in this huge house we stay.
Meet me in the middle,
at least once every day.

Actinomyces Israelii

The doctors could not catch it in time,
It disappeared quickly, tiny and diced,
From between my teeth that grind,
The open wound my bite guard sliced.
Systemic failure crippled me,
It ate away adjacent flesh,
Itchy eyes, I couldn't see,
Colonies where it liked to nest.
Deep within my bones,
Sealed up by natural process,
My body aches in silent moans,
Ongoing pain is horrendous.

Post-Traumatic Stress Disorder

I scream into my pillow
midnight's nightmares giggle
they whisper tauntingly
reminding me of the blast.
I kick free of the blankets
bedding plops on the floor
memories of the rotting dead
raving rancid in my head.
I scream out loud
slam my fist into the wall
my wife calls to comfort me
too ashamed to speak openly.
Echoes of my brothers
beckon me back
to the very scary moment
of the suicide attack.
Therapist chatters boringly
about the same old song
singing in my ears
all my brothers gone.

Hamid Karzai International
Airport Afghanistan

Alert!
Incoming rounds
Stop what you are doing.

Boom!
Incoming shells
Scent of gunpowder smoke.

Swoosh!
Incoming rockets
Damage on the airfield.

Help!
Medics run
Civilian crowd control.

Panic!
Push them back
Shelter in the bunkers.

Gasp!
Gates secure
Smoky clouds settle.

C-130

Sitting on the tarmac,
Round and hazy gray,
Propellers spinning,
To leave without delay.
Cargo-net seat straps,
Supports my body weight.
Battle gear tied up,
Secured for the flight.
Helmet buckled on,
With goggles pulled down
Buddies seated too,
Plane leaves the ground.
Call sign Papa Bear,
Radar contacts clear,
Except escort fighter,
Armed and flying near.
Casket in the back,
A fallen brother lies,
He's going home too,
After war for many days.

The Day of the Suicide Bomber

The streets of Kabul were wet with cool, misty rain,
I should have recognized the absence of people as a preattack indicator.
I continued on my journey because I had a wish.
The deafening shock of the blast rocked me into the wall.
Sudden smoky salmon swirls shifted in the air. Five local police
    disappeared.
I was furious at the mayhem because I had to delay my mission.

Medicated

Crippling back and leg pain
in agony, I am sober,
keeps me incapacitated
along with anxiety disorder,
soon I will be medicated
and dream about my horror.
My pills are long, fat, and blue
I take them every day,
I swallow one or two
and reality fades away,
mouth open, start to drool,
voices lead me astray.
Gray cemetery surrounds me
a prison for what I did,
with faith, I try to believe
God, he was just a kid,
his face in my sight I see
I squeezed, and it shook my bed.
Meds wearing off
shocked, alert, and awake,
heart beating rough
more pills I need to take,
such scary stuff
my dreary, painful fate.

My Military Retirement

Medals polished and shiny
reflect glints of the sun's shine,
dress blue buttons, polished gold
with gilded thread, so very fine.
Speeches of trumpeted triumphs
with blazing banners in hand,
our flag claps against the wind
drummers drive the marching band.
Two clanging bell strikes
times the end of the tour,
solemn walk down carpeted plank
"Sailor, going ashore!"
Etched ceremonial sword
above my bed on the wall,
sings to me sad melodies
of marching brave and tall.

Where We Lay

We lay where stone sentinels silently stand guard over forever beds
with glorious angels bearing shields in protection of the hallowed
    dead.
We lay where etched epitaphs cry out in a chorus of names
known only to those who visit our remains.
We lay where the caretaker's apprentice meanders on his appointed
    rounds
visiting each resident picking dead flowers from the grounds.
We lay waiting for you to join us, for we so desire
to hear a new voice in our eternal choir.

Ancient Earth

Hallowed home of all that live
Keeper of secrets long lost
Resting place of ancient hosts.
We live above and rest below
when we make our final bed
with stones above our heads.
We reach inside you to
fondle your treasures.
Weavers of gold, silver, and gems
suck your veins dry in greedy desire
for temporary delights.
Wasters of resources feast
on your creations.
Time but tickles thy visage
yet dooms our puny persistence.
Tell us a story
with pottery fragments
and bone.
Torment us for
failing to understand.
We live but a little while
on your eternal skin
dancing deliriously
never fitting in
until we lay down
arranged neatly
in the ground.

The Sword of Truth

Forged so long ago
by the archangels' might,
Defender of the Faithful
illuminous at night.

Passed from father to son
by blood right when fielded,
Gilded handle fits tight,
the wielder is shielded.

Blessed with special power
its splendor grows bright,
Dependable in the hour
when evil demons bite.
Designed as a part
of the faithful's mighty armor,
March forward in truth
onward Christian soldier.

Demons in the Dark

We hear your thoughts constantly
and lick the sweet taste of your sin.
We long in the dark for eternity
and grow strong by luring you in.

Your darkest desires are well known
when your free will becomes weakest.
We laugh because you think you own
worldly treasures that are the best.
Deny your Father's commandments
until your heart is black as coal.
Overcome the guilt
protecting your valuable soul.

Sign our contract freely, stating
our corporation will provide.
You will never end up hating
having chosen to join our side.

Now we own you for our purpose
you've had your temporary fun.
Submit is your only recourse
for there is no place you can run.

Regret your hasty decision
as you labor so deep below.
Free will was an illusion
our lies are all you know.

Escape

Heavy cave dirt packed so tight
Musty, dry dust fills the way
dim light in forever night
I miss the glory of the day.
Bitter ashes taste dreary
and float freely in the air
footprints show clearly
someone else has been there.
Jagged angled rock reaches
with points narrow and sharp
they defend the way, and it teaches
me to tread carefully in the dark.
Cold, wet trickles dance down
to muddy pools of water
where creepy insects found
a haven from their slaughter.
Disturbed bats beat their wings
and fly past me in a flutter
toward where the wind sings
and the caretaker's mutter.
At last, the exit grows nearer
I lost my bag of treasure
smooth surfaces act like a mirror
my complexion pale beyond measure.
Eyes squint at newfound light
I breathe in the chilly fresh air
snow falls white and bright
I'm free from depression's lair.

Ascending from Below

Ascension allows an account of my adventure
above the pit, I previously plummeted into
perilously persuaded by people of poor character.
Worldly treasures tricked me to taste temptation
with wicked whispers torturing my ears
telling me to take what I wanted whenever.
Buried beneath bounds of beautiful
Luxuries, I basked in bonds of deception where
devils dared me to dig deeper.
Darkness devoured distant dreams and
I felt the weight of my sin sink my soul
where in guilty silence, I saw a reaper.
Regret reminded me to repent
and seek salvation, so I surrendered
and asked for mercy from this disgrace.
Golden rays of glaring light pierced the darkness
allowing me to climb from the gloomy depths of despair
to feel the glow of God's glorious great sun upon my face.
Debris dropped down off my white gown, and I gripped
my solid staff stepping higher, having come so far
with heavenly hallows heroically up this hill.
Flags of freedom flap with flowing winds
where I wait for my friends to follow me
for I found my way with God's will.

Shine

Glow bright like a lamp on fire
chase after all you desire
Dance until your heart is free
lift your voice in song with me.

Salvation is in our grasp
if we only dare to ask
believe in the Promised Land
and march with the holy band.

Shine for others to see
in darkness, they need not be
Escape from the enemy
aboard a ship on the open seas.

ABOUT THE AUTHOR

BENJAMIN RICHARD ADDISON ROSE THROUGH the enlisted ranks as a US Navy illustrator and retired as a Lieutenant Commander public affairs officer after twenty-six years of active-duty service. He earned an associates degree in graphic design, a bachelor of science in communication, a master of arts in strategic security studies, and a master of fine arts in creative writing. He is a survivor of child abuse and continues to fight against post-traumatic stress disorder from his most recent deployment to Afghanistan.

Milton Keynes UK
Ingram Content Group UK Ltd.
UKHW030627280824
447491UK00001B/79